A Fishing Guide
to Kentucky's Major Lakes

A Fishing Guide to Kentucky's Major Lakes

by Arthur B. Lander, Jr.

Menasha Ridge Press
Hillsborough, North Carolina

© 1984 by Arthur B. Lander, Jr.
All rights reserved
Printed in the United States of America
Published by Menasha Ridge Press
Hillsborough, North Carolina

Book design by Lani Cartier
Maps by Karen Wysocki
Cover photo by Arthur B. Lander, Jr.

Library of Congress Cataloging in Publication Data
Lander, Arthur B.
  A fishing guide to Kentucky's major lakes.
  Includes index.
  1. Fishing—Kentucky—Guide-books. 2. Fishes,
Fresh-water—Kentucky. 3. Lakes—Kentucky—Guide-
books. I. Title.
SH499.L36 1984   799.1'1'09769   84–19060
ISBN 0–89732–023–9

Menasha Ridge Press
Route 3 Box 450
Hillsborough, NC 27278

*To Eugenia and Babe
and fishing Moms everywhere*

Contents

Acknowledgments

First of all, I would like to thank Bob Sehlinger of Menasha Ridge Press for giving me the opportunity to do this book.

Bob, when we first discussed the book, I could tell you were just as excited about it as I was. It makes an author's job that much easier when dealing with an understanding, dedicated and hard-working publisher. I appreciate the way you took time off from a busy work schedule to see that our business arrangement was completed quickly, so that I could begin writing.

I would like to thank Bonnie "Rhonda Jo" Brannin for her support during this laborious project. Bonnie, your energy level and talent are truly motivational. Your presence helped to sustain me through the final months of what was a two-year effort, off and on. I appreciate your understanding and concern during the summer and fall spent typing material into the system, editing and rewriting.

I feel deeply indebted to John Wilson, Director of Public Relations for Kentucky's Department of Fish and Wildlife Resources. Thanks for your help not only on this project but in gathering story material that eventually found its way into print as newspaper features and magazine articles. I think the overview you have provided me has made a considerable contribution to this book.

I also owe a debt of gratitude to the department's staff of fishery biologists, who have given good cooperation through the years. In no particular order, I would like to thank David Bell, in Calhoun; Bill McLemore, in Murray; Assistant Director and Dingell-Johnson Coordinator Jim Axon; bass biologist Gerry Buynak, and his fishery aide Shane Peck; predator biologist Benjy Kinman and Charlie Gorham, in Frankfort; Bonny Dale Laflin, in Bowling Green; Kerry Prather, in Prestonsburg; Assistant Director of Fisheries Ted Crowell, and Director of Fisheries Pete Pfieffer.

While the persons listed above helped me directly in this project, virtually everyone on the fisheries staff has at one time or another provided me with lake management background, program insight or population data. I appreciate everyone's cooperation.

While the job of a fishery biologist may seem like all fun, I know from experience that it can be cold, dirty and exhausting work. I've helped run a few gill nets in January before. I know that our state fishery biologists have a genuine concern for the rich resources of Kentucky's waters. They've proven to me that they are pledged to manage our fishes responsibly.

Thanks go out to the many anglers and conservation officers who provided me with details on tackle, techniques and seasonal tactics. A special thanks goes to Al Lindner, Billy Westmorland and Ron Shearer, all fishing experts in the truest sense of the word, for imparting their infinite wisdom on this ol' boy. If I've forgotten anyone, please accept my apology, and forgive me for the oversight.

Likewise, many thanks to the U.S. Army Corps of Engineers public affairs officers in the three districts I dealt with and the resource managers on the individual lakes. I would also like to thank Dr. Robert Hoyt at my alma mater, Western Kentucky University, for providing me with an excellent fisheries management background, which I hope is reflected in this book. A special thanks also goes out to Dave Wilkins for his leadership and positive mental attitude.

I would also like to say thanks to Susan Clore for introducing me to the TRS-80 Model III Microcomputer with Scripsit Word Processing program, on which the manuscript for this book was written. I tip my hat to the Tandy Corporation for producing such an excellent writer's tool.

And finally, I would like to thank Judy King, my typist, for working Saturdays and week nights, punching information into the system, at the beginning of this project.

Preface

Some of my fondest memories from childhood are of fishing on Herrington Lake. Those were special times in so many ways.

As a youngster, the mystique of dawn held its spell over me. It still does today. I look forward to those mornings on the lake when the backdrop of hills slowly appears through swirling mist, as the sun climbs high in the sky, burning off dense fog.

In adulthood, I realize that the time I spend on the lake is nourishment to my spirit and, oh, so soothing on the nerves. I suppose it's escapism, but there's something very marvelous about awakening at first light after a good night's sleep and going fishing.

During those childhood fishing trips, we would eat breakfast on the cabin's screened porch by the light of a bare bulb. From the darkened woods would come a raspy chorus of crickets and the echoing calls of birds—the haunting cry of the whippoorwill, the comic mimicry of "hoot" owls, the shrill scream of the screech owl. Sleepily, we'd make our way down to the dock.

The morning air was fresh and rejuvenating. So clean and sweet. If we had forgotten to stow the boat cushions away in the locker for the night, they'd be wet with dew. That didn't happen much, since Dad usually saw to it that our gear was in its place in our locker at the end of each day.

In summer, the mud daubers liked the locker too, and made their homes amid the rods and reels, tackle boxes, life jackets, charcoal grill, and my dad's Johnson Seahorse 10-horsepower outboard motor. We didn't bother the wasps if they didn't bother us.

As our flat-bottomed, wooden johnboat cut through the glassy waters, the reflections of towering rock cliffs along the shoreline wavered in the tiny wake. The hum of the outboard motor sometimes lulled me back to sleep in the mornings, as I lay on a blanket in the bottom of the boat.

We were a fishing family, and we spent as much time as possible together on the lake. It was one of the few places we really enjoyed each other's company. Our petty family arguments and gripes seemed to lose their importance when we got to the lake.

My dad collected driftwood, so he always kept a sharp eye out for something to take home as a memento of the trip—a delicate piece, bleached and smooth from years of exposure to water and sun. Cedar roots make the best driftwood, he always told me.

My mom and I did most of the fishing. We knew where practically every stump, submerged treetop and rock shelf was in the Cane Run Branch. We knew where to find crappie, bass or bluegill. Every now and then we got skunked, but not very often.

It's inevitable that all fishing kids grow up. Their years are measured by steadily increasing skills with rod and reel and chronicled in faded snapshots of broad grins behind full stringers of fish, taped to the refrigerator door. Looking back on these days, there is both joy and sadness.

The images and aromas are still vivid in my mind—the glistening turquoise and orange underbellies of longear sunfish, the warm glow of a gas lantern fending off the darkness and chill of the lake at midnight, the smell of crappie fillets frying in the skillet. And paramount in my emotions, the boyish craving for my first braggin'-size largemouth. That is the joy.

With the realization of those fishing dreams comes an ironic twist of fate, and a sadness of sorts. With age, and angling prowess, the enthusiasm and mystery that all beginning anglers know slip away. It seems harder and harder to recapture that spirit.

I suppose I want to go back to the days when we used a scull paddle instead of an electric trolling motor and we really thought luck had a lot to do with fishing. It was more fun then, I think.

I hope I will never lose touch with those feelings which were so much a part of fishing as a child. It's amazing how much fishing has changed just in my short lifetime. The sophistication of tackle and technique has brought with it a new competitiveness, and unheard-of angler success. It's my sincere hope that the fishermen of tomorrow will realize that the resource must come first. There are encouraging signs that this is happening, but there was a time when I wasn't quite sure it would.

The best way to get back to your fishing roots, and recapture the feelings all beginning anglers know, is to take a youngster fishing. You'll be surprised to find that your memories may become their memories too—and you may even relive a cherished part of your childhood.

What they learn from you will be more important than just how to run an outboard motor, rig a plastic worm or carve out fish fillets. They'll learn that to love is to teach and share.

Introduction

A Fishing Guide to Kentucky's Major Lakes was written primarily as a reference book, the definitive source of information on the locations, size, access highways, marina facilities and fishing opportunities of Kentucky's top sixteen impoundments. It is a tool for anglers planning trips afield in a state which is unparalleled for the mix of lake types and sport fishes.

There are deep, cold lakes, like those common in Canada, teeming with walleye, muskie and smallmouth bass, and there are shallow, mud-bottomed impoundments, typical of the South, famous for huge catfish, bluegill and largemouth bass. This mix of lakes is guaranteed to test the skill of any angler. I don't feel that I would be going out on a limb to say that it would take several lifetimes to learn all there is to know about fishing the lakes profiled in this book.

I don't pretend to be an "expert" on these lakes. I believe that the strength of this book is that many local anglers, guides, conservation officers, tournament fishermen and the biologists who manage these impoundments have contributed their knowledge and experience.

Time and space have placed restraints on just how much I could write on each lake, but working within those limits, I have tried to give an accurate overall picture of what type of fishing is best at each lake, where fish can be found during the various seasons of the year, and what the proven tackle and techniques are.

The book begins with a section on the twelve top sport fishes found in Kentucky. Emphasis here is on taxonomy, description, food habits, current Kentucky and International Game Fish Association (IGFA) all-tackle world records, fishing techniques, plus an overview of the management history of the species. It's amazing how many line-class record fish Kentucky has produced and how close many of our state records are to the all-tackle world records.

The second section consists of descriptions of the ten impoundments with more than five thousand surface acres and six selected "small" lakes. These smaller lakes are worthy of mention for a number of reasons. Dewey Lake, for example, has an emerging tiger muskie fishery. Greenbo Lake has yielded two state record largemouth. Herrington has been the site of intensive efforts to establish a "two-story" fishery.

The profile of each of the sixteen lakes, listed in alphabetical order, features the main sport fish available, although usually all of the sport fishes found in the lake are discussed somewhat. At the back of the book are line maps that show access roads, boat-launching ramps and marina locations and a table that summarizes boat-rental prices and availabilities.

It should be noted that some marinas listed here as being open year-round are really open in the off-season only in the sense that the manager lives on the premises and by special arrangement made by mail or over the phone visitors can have access to facilities. Even if the marina is listed as open year-round, it may not mean that there's some- one there every day. Space does not permit the mention of such facili- ties as campgrounds, motels or rental cabins at marina sites.

I have tried to be as comprehensive and correct as possible. Marina information was gathered from tourism publications and by telephone interviews; rental boat prices, of course, are subject to change without notice. If readers note any mistakes, we would appreciate knowing about them. Write in care of Menasha Ridge Press, Route 3, Box 450, Hillsborough, NC 27278, or telephone (919) 732-6661.

Bass fishing on Lake Cumberland—courtesy of Kentucky Department of Tourism

Major Lakes
of
Kentucky

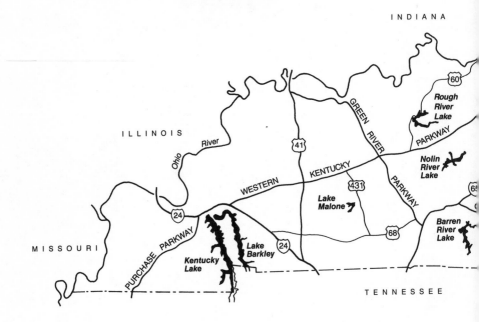

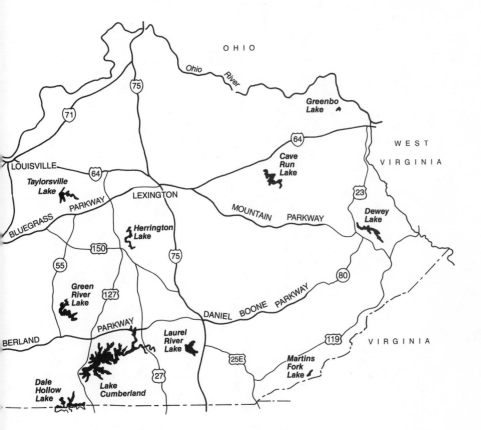

A Fishing Guide
to Kentucky's Major Lakes

Photo courtesy of Mercury Marine

The Fish

Bluegill

Even though the bluegill is one of America's most popular panfish, this scrappy gamester doesn't always get the respect he's due. There are some anglers who believe that the bluegill is nothing more than a forage fish.

And it's a shame too. Just because the bluegill lacks the size and glamour of other game fishes, he's certainly nothing to sneeze at. The bluegill's flesh is firm and sweet; he's one of our best-tasting fishes. Also, it's doubtful that bluegills could be landed on conventional bass-angling tackle if it was possible for them to grow as big as largemouths.

Adult bluegills are beautiful fish. Their coloration is variable, but generally they are olive green with emerald, copper, green and bluish reflections on their sides, dark above the lateral line. Their lower sides and belly are whitish to yellow. Sometimes big "hawg" bluegills have bright red underbellies.

Their geographic range extends from northeastern Mexico to Florida, north to the Great Lakes. The bluegill (*Lepomis macrochirus*) is a member of the family Centrarchidae and is the most widely distributed of the seven sunfishes of genus *Lepomis* found in Kentucky's largest man-made impoundments. Kentucky's top bluegill lakes are Kentucky Lake, Herrington Lake, Laurel River Lake, Lake Malone, Greenbo Lake and Green River Lake.

The current Kentucky state record bluegill, caught by Phil M. Conyers of Madisonville while bass fishing in a strip-mine lake, weighed four pounds, three ounces. The monster bluegill was caught on a spinning rod and reel and plastic worm. The IGFA all-tackle world record bluegill weighed four pounds, twelve ounces; it was caught in Ketona Lake in Alabama on April 9, 1950, by T. S. Hudson.

Bluegills feed mostly on insects, larvae, fish eggs, scuds, mollusks, worms and the fry of fishes; they have gluttonous appetites, which they never seem to satisfy. Bluegills are continuously on the move, except during the spawn, when they become fiercely territorial. They prefer shallow water throughout the spring and early summer, when they are most easily taken. Spawning occurs in late May or June when water temperatures reach into the 70s. Their nests are saucer shaped and clustered in colonies.

Extreme hot or cold weather tends to make bluegills, especially the larger fish, very selective in their food choices. For example, in summer the biggest bluegills go deep, and are usually taken in fifteen to thirty feet of water by drift fishing stair-step points, steep rock walls, deep-water holes, rock shelves, submerged boat houses, brush piles or tree-tops along the channel breakline.

To take big bluegills consistently, an angler must adapt his tackle and technique to seasonal wanderings and feeding preferences, just as in bass fishing. The expert bluegill angler may even fish with specialized rods, tipped with piano wire. Jigging the depths with grubs, flies or crickets is an effective technique for bottom fishing, as it imitates the natural action of benthic organisms.

The best live bait for bluegill fishing is crickets, red worms, bits of night-crawlers, meal worms, horseweed worms, bag worms, catalpa worms, grasshoppers and wax worms. Anglers forever searching for the one bait that will entice big bluegills have on occasion even tried maggots, wasp larvae, crayfish tails or tiny bits of salt-water shrimp baited on jigs. The ideal tackle for bluegills is ultralight spinning gear, four-pound test monofilament, and hooks of size 8, 10 and 12. Maribou jigs, 1/16-ounce curlytails, sinking flies such as the Skunk, size 16 dry flies and spinners like the 1/16-ounce Mepps Fury are excellent artificial lure choices.

Fly fishermen take huge stringers of bluegills in the early summer on poppers, nymphs, sponge spiders and rubber crickets. An expecially productive method for fishing for bluegills with spinning gear utilizes a clear bobber, one that resembles a "dummy" casting plug, except that it has an eyelet on each end. An 18-inch leader is tied to the rear eyelet. Dry and sinking flies work best on this rig; the weight of the clear bobber makes it easy to cast on light tackle. The "bobber and fly" rig is perfect for casting for bluegills when they head for open water during summer evenings, when the mayflies hatch.

To a lesser extent, several of the bluegill's cousins are found in Kentucky's lakes. The most common species are the longear sunfish, *Lepomis megalotis*; the redear sunfish or "shellcracker," *Lepomis micro-lophus*; and the green sunfish, *Lepomis cyanellus*. The shellcracker has been extensively introduced into the small lakes owned and managed by the Kentucky Department of Fish and Wildlife Resources, though it is found in only one lake profiled in this book, Lake Malone.

The longear sunfish is by far the second most common "bream" in Kentucky's lakes. This stream dweller is often found on rocky structure or at the headwaters of lakes in the old river channel. The bluegill is a superior competitor for food and cover in the lake environment, able to adapt considerably better than the green, longear, and redear sunfish.

Craigs Creek, Laurel River Lake—photo by author

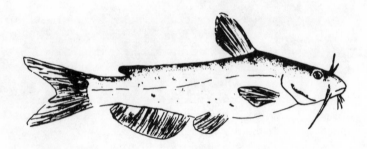

Catfish

Three species of catfish are most often caught by sport fishermen on Kentucky's man-made lakes—the flathead catfish (*Pylodictis olivaris*), the channel catfish (*Ictalurus punctatus*), and blue catfish (*Ictalurus furcatus*). All of these "whisker fish" are from the family Ictaluridae. The channel catfish is by far the most widely distributed.

The best fishing is in the tailwaters of Lake Barkley and Kentucky Lake, although catfish are abundant in the lakes with numerous flats—Dewey Lake, Barren River Lake, Green River Lake and Rough River Lake. Taylorsville Lake, by virtue of its forage base, bottom type and average depth, should be a good lake for catfish.

In early summer, June and July, the tailwater area below Kentucky Dam is in a class by itself, supporting unbelievable numbers of catfish, many of which are real monsters. The reason is the steady availability of forage fish—threadfin and gizzard shad, skipjack herring and minnows. The blue catfish predominates in the creel, and it's not uncommon for an angler to boat over 100 pounds of fish a day.

The situation is one of constant chumming. During the generation of electricity, many of these forage fishes are sucked through the intake and chopped up by the turbines; the catfish scavenge for their remains in the "boils." Thus, cut bait, preferably gizzard shad viscera and gills, is often very effective. Except for periods of cold weather in winter and bright sunlight in summer, shad can be dipped with an eight-foot long-handled dip net, as they school around riprap or bridge abutments.

To cut out the gills and viscera, (1) peel back and break the gill plates, (2) turn the fish on its back and make a quarter-inch cut behind the gills, (3) grab both gills between the thumb and forefinger and pull and (4) disembowel the shad by cutting with a knife from its anus through its body cavity. The bloody red meat of the gills and the smelly viscera are irresistible to big catfish.

Fishing tailwater areas requires the use of specialized gear—a heavy action rod, a spinning or casting reel spooled in 30-pound test mono-filament, a three-way swivel, a four-ounce sinker, a 1/0 hook, and a good depth finder so that rock piles, humpbacks and channel droplines can be located.

This rig is ideally suited to bottom-bouncing, since the sinker is attached by a leader to the lower rung of the three-way swivel, with the dropline trailing in the current. Keep the outboard motor running in forward just enough for a slow, controlled drift downriver.

Catfish will take a wide variety of baits—chicken livers, minnows, small bluegill, catalpa worms, prepared dough baits with a blood scent, nightcrawlers, crayfish, cut bait, and "stink baits," which appeal to the catfish's strong sense of smell.

These evil-smelling concoctions may be made from a number of revolting ingredients, such as chicken blood and intestines, carp dough, soap, cotton, clay and any number of kitchen preparations such as mustard and Limburger cheese. Often the ingredients are mixed up and left to get rancid in a jar with the top tightly screwed on. Many stink baits are the results of many years of experimentation and are guarded secrets.

The state record blue catfish weighed 100 pounds, and was taken from the Tennessee River below Kentucky Dam on August 21, 1970, by J. E. Copeland of Benton. The state record flathead catfish was also a monster, tipping the scales at 97 pounds. It was caught by Esker Carroll on June 6, 1956, from the Green River. The state record channel catfish weighed 22 pounds, 5 ounces, and was caught by Wallace Carter of Lawrenceburg on October 6, 1978, from a farm pond.

Catfish can occasionally be taken on artificial lures—plastic worms, flies, spinners and pork and jig combinations. It's uncommon for catfish to take artificials, since they prefer live bait, but it does happen.

Many techniques other than pole and line are adaptable to catfishing. The top-producing techniques are jug fishing shallow flats at night, limblines, and trotlines, both deep-water sets and bank-to-bank sets across narrow embayments. Quart and pint plastic bleach bottles, 40-pound test nylon line, and 1/0 or 2/0 gold hook are all that's needed for jug fishing. The light hooks will straighten out if you get hung, yet they're strong enough to hold a big catfish. Larger jugs seem to blow in the wind more, and they're harder for a catfish to take under, resulting in break-offs.

Fish in five to twelve feet of water for best results. Rock piles and rip-rap are excellent in the early summer during the spawning season, while later in the year the shallow, muddy flats adjacent to the deep water of the old river channel yield big fish. A strip of black friction tape wrapped around the jug will help keep your lines from tangling up—they make convenient hook-holders.

The limbliner ties his line to an overhanging tree limb, suspending the bait six to eight inches off the bottom. The ideal limb is one that can wear the fish down, absorbing enough of the power of his run to keep him from breaking off. Heavy nylon line and 2/0 hooks are suggested; always

Blue catfish taken below Kentucky Dam—photo by author

remember to secure the line behind a knot or branch of the limb, so that the catfish won't pull the line off the end of the limb when he power-dives. Don't tie your line on dead limbs, and be sure to check every line, even if it's not moving as you motor by. Catfish often give no tell-tale sign when they're hooked; they sulk between attempts to break loose.

The trotline fisherman attaches numerous "drops" to a main line, which is made from #18 to #24 nylon line. The short secondary lines from which the 3/0 stainless steel hooks dangle are made of doubled #7 nylon line; the "drops" are attached to the main line by barrel swivels, thus preventing twist in the line when a big fish is hooked. Using floats (plastic jugs or liter plastic soft drink bottles) and weights, the trotline can be set in open water at varying depths without its being tied to the bank.

In lakes the strategy is to intercept the fish as they migrate from deep to shallow water seasonally. Catfish seek out cooler water in the summer and warmer water in the winter. In spring, prior to the spawn, they'll be in the shallow embayments feeding on shad, crayfish or nightcrawlers. Shallow ridges off the old river channel and the flats at the mouths of the main creeks are tops as the fish spawn in late May and June. Summer and winter dictate deep-water sets.

Baits that are often used in the summer are shad viscera, sponge cheese, leeches and white raisins (sultanas). Blocks of white soap work well in the colder months of the year; when it gets warm they melt too fast. It's best to run your trotlines in the morning and afternoon. In the warm water of summer, with its low oxygen levels, hooked catfish will spoil in less than twelve hours. So it's important to run your lines faithfully around the clock.

Catfishing is fun and remarkably popular in Kentucky. The catfish may be short on looks, but he sure is tops at the dinner table, deep fried in cornmeal.

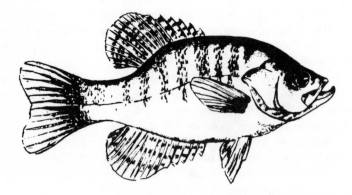

Crappie

The two species of crappie found in Kentucky are the white crappie, *Pomoxis annularis,* and the black crappie, *Pomoxis nigromaculatus.* These two members of the sunfish family, Centrarchidae, can be distinguished from one another by coloration and the number of dorsal spines.

The white crappie, commonly called newlight, has silvery olive shading to darker olive green on its back; it usually has six dorsal spines, but in rare cases has five. The black crappie, commonly known throughout the Deep South as the spec, or calico bass, is also silvery olive, but with dark green to black wormlike markings; the black crappie usually has seven or eight dorsal spines that are equal in length to the anal fins.

Both species of crappie are found in all river drainages of Kentucky. Thus, they are abundant in most of our man-made impoundments. They sometimes are even stocked in ponds and small state-owned lakes. Crappies feed on a wide variety of organisms, including invertebrates such as crustaceans and insects, but their diet is mostly small fishes. They are strictly carnivorous, and their preferred food is young-of-the-year minnows.

Crappie reach maturity in about three years. Their nests are shallow depressions in three to eight feet of water; they spawn in the spring when water temperatures reach into the 60s. One female may produce up to 100,000 eggs in one season.

The IGFA all-tackle world record for the white crappie is five pounds, three ounces. The fish was caught on July 31, 1957, at Enid Dam in Mississippi by Fred L. Bright. The all-tackle world record for black crappie is six pounds. Lettie T. Robertson caught this record calico bass on November 28, 1969, from Seaplane Canal in Westwego, Louisiana. Kentucky's state record crappie (our records make no distinction between the two species) is four pounds, three ounces, just one pound less than the white crappie all-tackle world record.

In Kentucky lakes, white crappies are generally more abundant than black crappie. Kentucky crappie anglers generally use live bait; commercially-available bluntnose and shiner minnows as well as hand-netted threadfin and gizzard shad minnows are popular. The crappie, one of the most sought after game fish in Kentucky, is taken on everything

Crappie—photo by author

from cane poles, to fancy telescoping fiberglass rods with piano wire tips, to ultralight spinning tackle.

Crappie prefer to school around cover—preferably stumps and brush on the edge of submerged creek channels or in flooded standing timber.

Kentucky Lake put crappie fishing on the map in our state and gave birth to a rig which allows an angler to fish two minnows at once, each at a different depth. One hook is tied to the end of the line. A one-ounce egg sinker is attached to the line ten inches above the hook, and a three-eyelet swivel is attached ten inches above the sinker, with a leader and hook suspended off of it.

Heavy line, preferably 20-pound test, and a 2/0 light wire hook is used, so that the hook will straighten out and the rig won't break when it's snagged on the bottom. The position of the sinker helps the angler jiggle loose the bottom hook when it's snagged. The rig is often used with a flyrod.

In April and May, the spawning season, crappie head for shallow water. They congregate under drift and shoreline brush submerged by high water. They are readily located in the spring, but in deep water during the hot months of summer and in winter they can be difficult to locate. This is when drift fishing comes into play. Once a couple of fish are taken from one spot, throw out a float marker and drift through the area again and again.

Knowing crappie movement throughout the year is the real key to angling success. You've got to find them to catch them. Crappie will usually bite all day, but tend to hit best early and late during hot weather and midday during winter. Crappie seem to bite best just before a front moves in and during a light rain. A drop in water level will virtually shut off crappie feeding sprees. A rise in water level usually means good fishing.

During the hottest months of summer and the coldest months of winter crappie utilize nearly the same areas. In flatland reservoirs like Kentucky Lake, Lake Barkley and Barren River Lake, crappie usually congregate in their deep-water haunts along the old river channel.

Crappie prefer smaller minnows in the winter. Progressively larger minnows work best through the year, although during the spawning run, when crappie are actively feeding, big, wiggly minnows will often work best. Cold weather sometimes makes crappie sluggish and their bites are subtle, requiring angler concentration and patience. Let them run with the bait; they may not smack it, but rather grab it and swim off.

During early spring and late fall, crappie move to the mouths of creeks. In mountain impoundments like Lake Cumberland or Dewey Lake crappie stay in relatively deep water, fifteen to thirty feet, most of the year. In flatland reservoirs, the early spring and late fall patterns are identical. The best fishing is adjacent to deep water, especially stump and brush clusters on the breakline. If you bounce your minnow or jig on the ridge flats, you might just catch a spotted bass, a sauger, or even a freshwater drum, nicknamed "sheephead," "white perch," or "Gasper Goo."

Hydrographic maps and a depth finder are almost always needed to pinpoint such potential hotspots. In our best lakes, finding crappie is no problem. All of the lakes profiled in this book have crappie in them except Lake Malone, Greenbo Lake and Martins Fork Lake. They were never stocked in these smaller lakes.

If you're really after lots of big crappie, the lakes in western Kentucky are the best producers. If there's a sleeper crappie lake in the state, it's Cave Run Lake.

The hard part about crappie fishing comes when it's time to clean a limit of sixty big slabs. The eating takes care of itself.

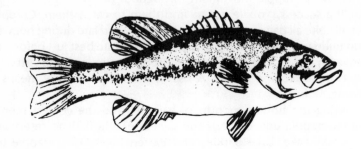

Largemouth Bass

The largemouth bass, *Micropterus salmoides*, is the most abundant bass in Kentucky's man-made impoundments. "Ol' Bigmouth" knows every trick in the book to throw a lure; he's a terrific brawler in close quarters, able to break even the stoutest monofilament with sudden dives and gill-rattling acrobatics.

The state record largemouth weighed 13 pounds, 10 ounces, and was caught on April 14, 1984, from Wood Creek Lake in Laurel County by Dale Wilson of Swiss Colony. The IGFA all-tackle world record large-mouth, which weighed twenty-two pounds, four ounces, was caught on June 2, 1932, from Montgomery Lake in Georgia by George W. Perry.

Largemouth bass, a highly predacious fish, prefer forage fishes as their main food, though small water snakes, frogs, crayfish and insect larvae occasionally become part of the largemouth's diet. The largemouth bass is "America's Fish," beloved because of its availability, palatability and vicious strike, one of the most thrilling in fresh-water angling.

The most adaptable and highly available of the three species of "black basses" found in Kentucky, the largemouth can withstand and thrive in water conditions that would not support other species. By seeking out runoff water in spring they often avoid periods of low dissolved oxygen caused by "turnovers." They escape summer's high surface water tem-peratures by suspending deep in bands of water within their optimal temperature range. In Lake Cumberland, for example, the largemouth head for deep water in the summer and literally disappear from the bassman's creel.

Biologists from the Kentucky Department of Fish and Wildlife Re-sources raise largemouth at the Minor E. Clark Fish Hatchery near More-head, but these fish are used for stocking ponds and small community watershed lakes. No largemouth are stocked in Kentucky's major lakes; populations are sustained by natural reproduction.

Fishery biologists estimate that it takes two to two and one-half years on the average for a largemouth bass to reach the harvestable size of twelve inches in Kentucky. In some highly productive bodies of water in the western part of the state, however, the combination of a milder climate, longer growing season and massive forage base helps the large-mouth grow faster.

The largemouth is easily distinguished from the smallmouth. The largemouth's mouth is considerably larger, and the upper jaw extends well behind the eye. In addition, the spinous and soft portions of the dorsal fin, separate on the largemouth, are connected on the smallmouth.

Although the largemouth's color characteristics are similar to those of the spotted bass, the largemouth usually lacks the rows of conspicuous black dots below the lateral streak. The head of the spotted bass is more pointed and pikelike in appearance. The largemouth also lacks the small patch of burrlike teeth on the tongue, one of the more easily distinguished physical differences between the spotted bass and his cousin.

Largemouths are taken with a greater variety of techniques and tackle than any other freshwater fish. Popping bugs, crankbaits, plastic worms, jig and pork chunk combinations, spoons, surface propeller-type stick baits and spinnerbaits all take their share of largemouth bass.

In thirteen of the sixteen impoundments profiled in this book, it's possible for anglers to catch three species of bass—the largemouth, smallmouth and spotted—where their habitats overlap. No matter how hard an angler may fish for one of the three species, he will probably catch the others. In Martins Fork Lake, it's possible to catch four species of bass, since the impoundment also supports redeye bass, *Micropterus coosae.*

Winter's frigid water temperatures slow down the largemouth's metabolism, but it certainly doesn't shut off completely the urge to feed. Many of the largest fish of the year are taken in December, January and February by patient, knowledgeable anglers. The pig and jig combination is the top winter lure; black is the top color; and eels, frogs, split tails and ripple rinds are all used extensively.

Jig fishing is an extremely productive method for early spring, when rains muddy up the headwaters of lake embayments. The tackle is simple, yet very effective, and the action is fast. The jigging pole is usually a two-piece, telescoping fiberglass rod ten to fourteen feet in length. A small reel is often used to store extra line, and there's an eyelet through which the line is threaded. If you can't find one of these fancy rigs, a stout cane pole will do the trick.

The three to four feet of line should be at least 40-pound test, and heavy 4/0 to 8/0 hooks are recommended. Place a stationary cork 18 to 24 inches above the hook. The heavy hook and line are needed to withstand the extreme tension a big fish can exert in close quarters. A squirming gob of nightcrawlers is best in muddy water, a shiner in slightly clearer water. Jig fishing has been the undoing of many a lunker. The muddier the water, the shallower you should fish.

Big, prespawn female bass love to lurk in and around heavy cover in

Outdoor writer Wade Bourne with a 4-pound largemouth bass—photo by author

the early spring. Jigging is one of the best techniques for teasing them out of logjams, treetops and stump roots. The shallow-water bass technique called jigger-bobbin', popular in the Deep South, is similar to jig fishing, yet it's usually done at night. Buzzbaits, bucktails, popping bugs and spinnerbaits are dragged back and forth next to stumps and other likely looking cover.

Spring fishing calls for tactics that take advantage of the fact that bass are actively feeding to stockpile energy for the upcoming spawn. Medium-running crankbaits and top-water lures are a good choice.

Bass are constantly cruising the shallows, gorging themselves on any creatures hapless enough to be washed into the lake by heavy rains. Spinnerbaits are especially productive when the water is murky to muddy and up high in the weeds and shoreline brush. A stop-and-go bottom-bouncing routine or a steady retrieve over stumps and through flooded treetops is sure to catch fish this time of the year.

In summer, according to the books, bass angling becomes a search for water in the high 60s and low 70s. But, realistically speaking, bass do not always retreat into deep water. In Lake Barkley, it's not uncommon to catch bass in three feet of water on a surface lure during the summer.

The plastic worm is tops on most Kentucky impoundments during the summer. Fish the points, brush piles and creek channel droplines. Night fishing is the only way to really catch bass in numbers on most of our lakes during hot weather, especially the deep, clear ones. The Mann 6-inch augertail worm in electric grape is my personal favorite. I Texas rig it on a #2 Mister Twister worm hook, and an ⅛-ounce bullet sinker. Bass lights (blacklights) are necessary equipment for the serious night fisherman; the low light level doesn't seem to bother the fish, even those in just a couple of feet of water. These lights make working the banks trouble free, by helping anglers avoid hang-ups and short casting. The fluorescent lines glow in the blacklights, so anglers can detect even the slightest twitch.

Vertical jigging Hopkins or Blakemore spoons around bridge abutments and steep rock walls is another effective technique for summer suspended bass. Deep-running crankbaits are especially productive when fished across points in the summer at night. It's not uncommon to catch a big fish on the surface, too, by casting buzzbaits or black spinnerbaits. The Model-A Bomber, Rebel Wee-R, and Rebel Shad are top crankbaits.

In the fall of the year when water temperatures begin dropping, bass feed voraciously in sprees to fatten up for the long winter. The action is often brief, but fast and furious. Bass can be taken at almost any depth, and a variety of lures produce well after the lake turns over. Because of alternating periods of hot and cold weather, the best fishing may be delayed well into December. The deeper the lake, the longer it takes for the water to cool down into the 60s.

Large schools of largemouths attack schools of shad minnows. The shad are ganged up on, and the bass usually come out on top, feeding heavily in a relatively short span of time. When the schools of largemouths tear into the shad, boiling and churning the water much as white bass do, they are vulnerable to almost any shadlike lure, spoon or injured-minnow imitation tossed into the melee.

Largemouth bass—courtesy of Kentucky Department of Fish and Wildlife Resources

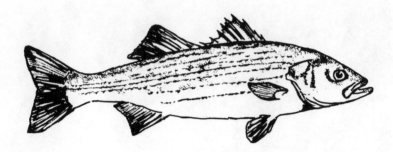

Rockfish

Kentucky's rockfish stocking program was conceived and initiated by Charlie Bowers during his tenure as director of fisheries for the Kentucky Department of Fish and Wildlife Resources. While the program never lived up to expectations, it was nonetheless one of the real success stories of fishery management in Kentucky. If you don't believe so, just look at the record books.

A saltwater relative of the white bass, the rockfish (*Morone saxatilus*) is a member of the true bass family, Serranidae. The rockfish closely resembles the white bass, but its body form is more elongated and less compressed, with nearly a straight back. Its coloration is dark greenish to bluish above, sometimes with a brassy tinge, becoming paler on its sides and silvery below. The predominant feature of the fish is seven to eight narrow longitudinal stripes. Its true common name is striped bass.

The rockfish stocking program has been a real shot in the arm for angling opportunities in Kentucky. From the first twelve rockfish taken by hook and line in 1957 from the Santee-Cooper Reservoir in South Carolina and stocked in Lake Cumberland, the project has grown immensely. Originally an anadromous species (living in salt water but spawning in fresh water), this native of the Atlantic and the Gulf of Mexico became land-locked in coastal reservoirs.

In the five years after the initial stockings in Kentucky, 2,792 more rockfish, many of them under thirteen inches were introduced into Herrington Lake, Lake Cumberland and Kentucky Lake. The stocking of rockfish fry began in 1965 when 540,000 were placed in Lake Cumberland. During those early years fry were also introduced into Dewey Lake, Lake Malone, the Ohio River, Lake Barkley and Green River Lake. After 1969 almost all rockfish introduced into Kentucky waters were fingerlings. Although biologists realize that fingerlings have a better survival rate than fry, there is the problem of die-offs due to temperature variables in brooder ponds at hatcheries.

In the past few years several rockfish in the thirty-pound class have been taken from Lake Cumberland, and biologists believe that most of these fish were from the 1969 stocking class. Scale samples sent in by anglers go a long way in helping biologists study the age and growth of these remarkable fish.

A 24- and 29-pound rockfish taken in the spring by Stu Tinney of Striper *magazine— courtesy of* Striper *magazine*

The rockfish program in Kentucky entered a new era in the summer of 1978 when the acquisition of broodfish was made easier by a netting operation. Biologists began raising fry from captured fish, inducing mature males and females to spawn in circular tanks, because rockfish don't spawn naturally in Kentucky waters. Thus, the program became independent, as biologists no longer had to rely on outside sources for rockfish fry.

A mature female rockfish that weighs thirteen pounds will produce approximately 1.5 million eggs. This means that the output of several fish easily supplies the number of fry introduced into Kentucky waters as fingerlings each year, thus accelerating the program for the future.

Feeding almost exclusively on gizzard shad (98 percent of their diet), rockfish are a valuable predator fish because they grow big enough to take fish that are too large for other predator species. Studies have proven that rockfish almost never eat bass.

The rockfish is an outstanding sport fish. They are big, brawny fish that take line in long, screeching runs, but surprisingly they usually die after being boated. Trolling or casting in the jumps with large shadlike crankbaits is a top angling method. Some fishermen swear by the use of live bluegills or vertical jigging Blakemore spoons and big jig and pork ripple rind combinations atop humpbacks along submerged river channels. The use of a graph recorder is a big help in locating marauding schools of rockfish, since they are pelagic—that is, they live and feed in open water—and are seldom caught next to the shore.

The current state record is 47 pounds, taken on November 28, 1979, by Forest Reed of Monticello, from Lake Cumberland. Kentucky's largest lake has also yielded an IGFA line class world record for 8-pound test. The 45-pound, 8-ounce rockfish was taken April 17, 1978, by Walter C. Lilly of Milton, West Virginia.

Today, rockfish fisheries are known to exist in Herrington Lake and Lake Cumberland, as well as below Kentucky Dam and Barkley Dam. As a point of comparison, consider that creel surveys on Lake Cumberland indicate that 9,000 pounds of rockfish were caught in 1980, compared to 165,000 pounds of crappie and 37,500 pounds of bass.

At the end of 1981, stockings in Lake Cumberland were ended, and the program has entered an evaluation phase that is expected to continue for another three years. The immediate objective of the rockfish stocking program is to increase the total harvest of rockfish by 10 percent to about one pound per acre or twenty-five tons annually, a realistic expectation based on the experiences of other states.

The long-term reasons for stocking rockfish are basically (1) benefit as sport fish, (2) predator value as "biological control" for runaway gizzard shad populations and (3) an alternative to the largemouth bass, to siphon off some pressure on bass populations.

Other lures that are ideal for vertical jigging are the bucktail jigs, rubber-tailed jigs, Bomber Slab spoons, Cordell spot, Gay Blade and Heddon Sonar. Some excellent trolling lures include the jointed Rebels, Bomber, Striper A, Hellbenders and Fliptail Flirts.

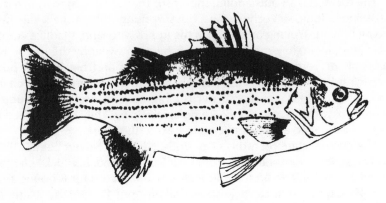

Rockfish–White Bass Hybrid

The rockfish–white bass hybrid is Kentucky's newest predator fish. Noting that it is referred to as the "Sunshine Bass" in Florida, and "Whiterock Bass" in Georgia, John Wilson, director of public relations for Kentucky's Department of Fish and Wildlife Resources, once jokingly suggested that we should call the fish stocked here "Bluegrass Bass." Why not? By whatever name, this fish is a legend in the making, and is sure to be around for years to come.

The "Bluegrass Bass" is an example of interspecific hybridization, the crossing of two species. Eggs are taken from the female rockfish (*Morone saxatilus*) and mixed with the milt of the male white bass (*Morone chrysops*). The result is a fish that typically exhibits hybrid vigor—it has a faster growth rate than either of the parent species, survives better in the hatchery and throughout the rigors of stocking and, to the angler's delight, is more catchable.

Surprisingly, interspecific hybridization among freshwater fishes often produces a fertile offspring. This is the case with the rockfish–white bass cross. The only drawback, if it can indeed be considered so, is that identification isn't always easy.

While the white bass has a deeper body and arched back, one patch of teeth on the back of the tongue, and faint body lines with only one extending to the tail, the hybrid has a more streamlined body with two patches of teeth on the back of the tongue and dark body lines with several extending to the tail. You would have little difficulty in distinguishing between the white bass and hybrid when you can see them side by side, but consider a cross between the two!

The rockfish–white bass hybrid was first introduced into Herrington Lake because the purebred rockfish failed to adapt. It was also hoped that the new bass would bolster the declining white bass fishery, which for years massed in the lake's headwaters on the Dix River for the annual spring spawning runs. The hybrid seems to do best in southern reservoirs, where conditions are somewhere between optimum white bass environments and optimum rockfish environments.

The first stockings were in 1979 when 38,000 of these remarkable "shad eating machines" were released in Herrington. In 1981, 83,000 more fingerlings were placed in the lake. All of the fish came from

Rockfish–white bass hybrid—courtesy of Kentucky Department of Fish and Wildlife Resources

Florida, and were traded to us for walleye. The 1982 stocking class totaled 250,000 fish. In both 1979 and 1981, the hybrids were also stocked in Barren River Lake.

With the new fish came new regulations (adopted in August 1982) which established a daily limit of 20 fish, only five of which can be over fifteen inches in length. As larger and larger "Bluegrass Bass" are taken, the state record continues to go upward. At this writing, Louis J. Maschinot of Villa Hills holds the state record with a 12 pound, 10 ounce fish taken on September 22, 1982, from the Ohio River at Mendahl Dam.

The rockfish–white bass hybrid that Maschinot caught was probably one of the thousands of fish stocked in the Ohio River by the West

Virginia Division of Fisheries in the mid-1970s. Migrations of rockfish–white bass hybrids have been well documented through tagging studies, so it's not unreasonable to assume that this fish could have traveled downriver a hundred miles from where it was released.

The IGFA world all-tackle record weighed 20 pounds, and was caught by Don Raley from the Savannah River near Augusta, Georgia, in 1977. Kentucky's first state record rockfish–white bass hybrid was caught at Herrington Lake on May 21, 1982, by M. J. Cleveland of Waddy. The fish weighed three pounds, eight ounces, and was 20⅜ inches long; predator biologist Benjy Kinman determined by scale aging that the fish was from the 1979 stocking class.

Sauger

The sauger is a member of the family Percidae, the perches and darters. The sauger and walleye closely resemble one another, and are often misidentified by fishermen. Both are found in all of Kentucky's major rivers, so consequently they are caught from the impoundments created by these rivers.

Sauger are cold-water fishes that begin their spawning run in February at a time when the warm-water species are still inactive. They live and feed on or near the bottom, yet it's a misconception that they are found only in deep water and that specialized fishing techniques are needed to catch them. I have caught respectable-size sauger in the two-pound class in as shallow as eight feet of water on ultralight spinning gear. Sauger are easy.

The increased turbidity of rivers, the blocking of spawning routes by high-rise dams, and a general lowering of water quality in such important rivers as the upper Cumberland, Tennessee, Kentucky and Barren have severely limited the sauger's range.

At one time the sauger was an important game fish in Kentucky. The annual runs were a grand occasion. Of course this was before Kentucky's major impoundments were built, and almost all angling was done in rivers. Sadly, most fishermen today know very little about the sauger and how to catch him. Sauger are a neglected resource. In addition, cold-water fishing isn't terribly popular here, but fishing strategies and techniques utilized throughout the Great Lakes states are highly effective here. If you can catch walleyes "up north," you can master the sauger.

It's not easy to distinguish between a walleye and a sauger. They are so closely related that the two fish are capable of mating, in fact, and producing a "saugeye" hybrid. The walleye has a whitish lower lobe on the caudal fin, and the sauger doesn't.

The sauger also has a black spot on the basal portion of the pectoral fin, saddlelike blotches on the body, and, internally, five to eight pyloric caeca (fingerlike structures where the intestines leave the stomach), versus three for the walleye. The sauger, *Stizostedion canadense*, is a smaller cousin of the walleye.

Al Linder with limit of sauger—photo by author

He's excellent tablefare, and, like the walleye, this slender, toothy fish travels in schools. When you take one sauger, there's a good possibility that there are others in the area. The sauger is rapidly gaining popularity among fishermen, especially those who fancy trolling.

The state record sauger was taken from Kentucky Lake. It weighed six pounds, one ounce and was caught by William H. Price of Murfreesboro, Tennessee, on July 26, 1972. The IGFA all-tackle world record sauger weighed eight pounds, twelve ounces and was taken by Mike Fisher on October 6, 1971, from Lake Sakakawea in North Dakota.

Sauger are taken in great numbers from the lower Tennessee and Cumberland rivers and Kentucky Lake. The en masse migrations to the tailwaters of dams on these two rivers have produced the best sauger fishing in the South. Pickwick Dam in central Tennessee is *the* sauger hotspot for the entire basin, but the dams on the Ohio River compare favorably.

The tailrace areas below Nolin River Lake, Rough River Lake, Herrington Lake, Barren River Lake, Martins Fork Lake and Laurel River Lake are known to support a limited sauger fishery. The hotspot in eastern Kentucky, though, is Wolf Creek Dam on the Cumberland River, in February, especially when the generators are off.

In summer, sauger are taken by deep-water trolling and night fishing with minnows in the Barkley Canal. Good catches of sauger are also taken each spring below Kentucky and Barkley dams in the discharge by casting jigs. Be sure to be "bottom-bouncing." Fuzzy grubs in fluorescent orange and yellow, baited with shiners, are especially effective.

Tailwaters are especially productive because they halt upstream migration and concentrate fish. Likewise, flatland reservoirs are predictable: fish the flats at creek mouths, and you'll never be too far off fish, and most of the times you'll be on top of them! Sauger can certainly light up a depth finder.

The sauger experts in Kentucky's waters have perfected a unique trolling method in which a 16-ounce elongated sinker is attached to one eyelet of a three-eyelet swivel. To the horizontal eyelet a stout leader and minnowlike lure are attached. No rod is used; instead, the line is simply stored on an automatic fly reel which is attached to the boat with a C-clamp. The heavy sinker keeps the lure down deep.

Steel line or heavy braided line is preferred, and the rig is hand fished. Even the most subtle strikes can be felt when the line is in your hand. Hooked fish are simply brought in hand over hand, the slack taken up with the reel. Sometimes spinners and spoons, instead of shadlike crankbaits, are trolled. The secret of success is keeping the lure right on the bottom where sauger feed.

Silver Muskellunge

The silver muskellunge, *Esox masquinongy ohioensis*, is the largest member of the pike family, Esocidae. One of three subspecies, the silver muskie's geographic range is from South Carolina and Tennessee north through the Mississippi River system into the Great Lakes region and Canada.

A moderately elongated, subcylindrically shaped fish, the muskie has a jaw shaped like a duck's bill and armed with numerous sharp teeth. The olive greenish back usually has black vertical bars; the belly is white.

The most important development in muskie fishing in Kentucky came in 1973 when the Minor E. Clark Hatchery below Cave Run Dam was completed and Kentucky Department of Fish and Wildlife biologists began raising these predator fish for an extensive stocking program in both streams and selected lakes.

The Licking River has always been muskie rich, more so than any other drainage in Kentucky. The muskie "hunters" of the old days were a hardy crew indeed, and their exploits are legendary. The section of the river that is now Cave Run Lake was the stomping grounds of perhaps the most die-hard group of these early muskie anglers, "The Lost Creek Musky Clan."

Prior to the opening of Cave Run Lake, the state didn't have an impoundment managed primarily for muskie. In the late 1960s and throughout the 1970s there were only limited stockings of muskie when they were available in trades from hatcheries in other states. In those days only fry were available for stocking, and their survival rate, which was none too good, had little, if any, effect on boosting native populations.

With the establishment of a rearing program, it became feasible to begin stocking not only in Cave Run but in other lakes that had adequate habitat and forage base. Now that muskie are being raised up to fifteen inches before stocking, their survival rate is much better.

Induced to spawn by hormones, the brood fish are stripped of their eggs and milt. After fertilization, the eggs are placed in aerated "hatching jars." After the larval fish absorb their yolk sacks, the fry are reared in brooder ponds.

Stocking muskie at an intermediate size means that there's less chance they'll be preyed upon by other game fishes. Muskie grow amazingly fast, as much as eleven inches their first year, which means that they become predators relatively early in life. Through age and growth studies and scale aging, Kentucky Department of Fish and Wildlife biologists have determined that it takes between three and four years for a muskie to reach harvestable size of thirty inches in Cave Run Lake. They attain a length of eighteen inches at two years of age, and twenty-four inches at three.

The availability of large numbers of fingerlings (a mature muskie female can produce upwards of 115,000 eggs) has made massive stockings in Cave Run Lake, Dewey Lake and Green River Lake possible. Usually, muskie are stocked at the rate of one fish per acre. For example, about 8,000 muskie are introduced into Cave Run Lake each spring, although in 1979, 14,800 eight-inch intermediates were released in the lake, the largest number stocked during any one year.

According to creel survey statistics, the muskie fishery in Cave Run Lake began to develop in 1975, peaked in 1976, and then began a slow decline in 1977. In 1976 an estimated 1,029 muskie were harvested. The lake record muskie weighed 41 pounds and was caught by Don Offil, of Mt. Olivet. While the lake continues to produce many trophy-class adults, the population dynamics of man-made impoundments are such that competition, fishing pressure and decreased productivity always lead to declines in sport fishes after the initial postimpoundment boom.

Muskie have strict habitat requirements. They prefer cool water in the range of 35 degrees Fahrenheit in winter to 78 degrees Fahrenheit in summer. Since they depend primarily on sight for locating food, they cannot tolerate turbid waters. Also, excessively high water temperature will cause them to stop feeding.

Muskie spawn from late March through the end of April, when water temperatures are between 54 and 60 degrees. They do not build nests and are believed to deposit their eggs in shallow areas where the bottom is decayed leaves, detritus or brush. The male and female fish swim side by side and deposit milt and eggs simultaneously. Cold spells and the quantity and quality of small forage fishes and zooplankton are limiting factors in the survival of their young.

Kentucky's state record muskie weighed 43 pounds, and was caught from Dale Hollow Lake on March 13, 1978, by Porter Hash of Edmonton. The record fish is claimed jointly by the states of Kentucky and Tennessee. The IGFA all-tackle world record muskie weighed 69 pounds, 15 ounces, and was caught by Art Lawton in New York in September 1957 from the St. Lawrence River.

Muskie are by far the most exciting predator fish in Kentucky, as far as

I'm concerned. They are vicious fish that delight in gorging themselves on suckers and carp in the shallows at the head of lake embayments in the spring. During the hot summer months they disperse into open water and suspend on the breaklines of submerged river channels, ripping into schools of twelve-inch gizzard shad that venture too close to their hiding places.

Muskie are loners who attack their prey from hiding. They prefer deadfalls, flooded standing timber and downed logs; muskie will follow a lure for some time before striking, so pinpoint casting isn't as important as it is in bass fishing, for example. More often than not, follow-ups don't necessarily mean strikes—or hooked fish.

The power runs and cartwheeling jumps of muskie help to tide the angler over from fish to fish, which may be weeks of steady fishing. Muskie fishing requires PMA (positive mental attitude). The hours are long and the frustrations many. But the next cast might be the one that rolls a trophy; there are definitely psychological aspects to muskie fishing.

Only the heaviest tackle is appropriate for muskie fishing. My rig is a 5½-foot Garcia model 8320 casting rod with very heavy taper Ambassadeur 5001 C level-wind casting reel spooled in black 30-pound test braided line. I tie a black, 12-inch, 30-pound test wire leader on the end of my line because muskie have sharp, pointed teeth, and break-offs would be common otherwise. The reason I use braided line rather than monofilament is that monofilament stretches under tension, which can make setting the hook all the more difficult.

Muskie are taken by trolling, casting and still-fishing with live bait. Some of the best lures for casting are bucktail spinners, top-water propeller baits, the Hawg Wobbler, Creeper, Suick jerk baits, buzzbaits like the Lunker Lure, and huge Mister Twister spinnerbaits (white with rubber, rippletail trailers). Spinnerbaits and buzzbaits should be equipped with trailer (stinger) hooks. Rubber surgical tubing prevents the hook from swinging too freely and causing hang ups.

Trolling is an especially effective postspawn muskie-angling technique. Flashy crankbaits like the Bagley, Hellbender, Rebel Shad and wobbling, injured-minnow imitations are top lure choices. The preferred color patterns are white and silver, orange and black, or light yellow and white. Be sure to troll along channel breaklines or across submerged humpbacks adjacent to deep water.

A steady, fast retrieve is preferred when casting because muskie like fast-moving targets and can be intimidated into striking. The fast retrieve also insures good solid hooking. The "figure 8" shouldn't be overlooked, since there are many follow-ups in muskie fishing. Once you get the

Selection of muskie lures—photo by author

lure to the boat, simply move the rod tip in a sweeping figure-8 motion, allowing the lure to slosh atop the water alongside the boat. You'll be surprised how many times a muskie will appear on the surface and snap at your lure. Be alert and ready for action. A big muskie hooked at the boat is a tall order to handle.

Don't forget that the winter months of December, January and February are prime muskie fishing weather; that's the time when many real whoppers are caught. A tried and true technique for early spring is jigging the banks with live bait—golden redhorse suckers, hog mollies (northern hogsuckers) and twelve-inch carp or goldfish.

Especially effective during the sucker spawn, this technique requires a stout pole, heavy line and hooks, and buckets of nerve. Quietly electric motor around promising cover, leading the bait through deadfalls and undercut banks. Imagine horsing a thirty-pound muskie into the boat on the end of a pole and short line. This technique was especially popular with the old-timers who fished the Licking River prior to the impoundment of Cave Run Lake.

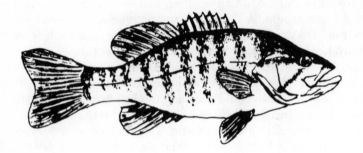

Smallmouth Bass

Kentucky is a smallmouth bass fisherman's dream come true.

Because the Bluegrass State is one of the southernmost states in the smallmouth's geographic range, bronzebacks grow just about as big in Kentucky as they do anywhere in the United States. In fact, Kentucky's state record smallmouth, an 11-pound, 15-ounce lunker taken from Dale Hollow Lake on July 9, 1955, by David L. Hayes of Leitchfield, is the current IGFA all-tackle world record for the species.

The smallmouth bass is indigenous throughout the area between eastern Iowa and the Appalachians, southward to Kansas, eastern Oklahoma and the Tennessee River system, northward throughout the Great Lakes region and Quebec. Through stockings, the smallmouth can now be found in waters from coast to coast.

A member of the sunfish family, Centrarchidae, the smallmouth bass, *Micropterus dolomieui*, is greenish with a bronze luster, belly silvery. The dark vertical bars are most conspicuous in fingerlings; on the cheek and opercle three bronze streaks radiate from the eye.

The smallmouth is considered by many anglers to be the cream of the crop of freshwater sport fishes. A fat and sassy bronzeback in the five-pound class is a prize that any sportsman can feel proud to have mounted. I'd much rather catch a two-pound smallmouth on ultralight spinning gear than a six-pound largemouth on a casting rod and reel any day of the week.

Smallmouth are more particular in their feeding habits than the largemouth and even the spotted "Kentucky" bass. The smallmouth's preferred food is crayfish, small minnows and shiners, hellgrammites, shad, mad toms, and salamanders, all of which can easily be seined from small creeks. Nightcrawlers are also a top smallmouth bass bait.

Remember that nothing beats live bait. Fishing minnows with just a small split shot on the line to keep the bait down is a deadly technique. One trick that pays off handsomely is clipping the pectoral or pelvic fin from one side of a minnow. This will cause the minnow to swim about erratically, looking as though it's crippled. This drives smallmouth crazy.

More important, smallmouth are highly selective about the size of their prey, so anglers should fish with smaller artificial lures and bait than they would normally use when going after largemouths, for example. Tiny lures from ¹⁄₁₆ to ¼ ounce and spiderweb-thin line (4- to 8-pound test monofilament) are commonly used when fishing for "hawg" bronzebacks. Spinnerbaits, pig and jig combinations, 4- and 6-inch plastic worms and crankbaits also give good results. I have caught keeper smallmouths out of Herrington Lake on propeller-type surface lures in the fall.

Some smallmouth are caught by accident by anglers fishing deep water for big spotted bass. The main reason why anglers fishing exclusively for smallmouth favor ultralight tackle is that these fish usually live in clear-water lakes. They spook easily, and the trophy-size fish are extremely wary. Heavier tackle is used primarily when fishing extremely deep water, which these fish often seek out, or when fishing shallow water in heavy cover at night. This last technique is highly productive at Dale Hollow Lake on those rare occasions when the lake is on the rise in the fall.

The huge impoundments of the upper Cumberland and Obey rivers, Lake Cumberland and Dale Hollow Lake, respectively, are Kentucky's top smallmouth bass waters, although Green River Lake isn't far behind. Smallmouths in the six-to-eight-pound class are taken from these three lakes each year. Recently, smallmouth bass fisheries are growing in Barren River Lake, Kentucky Lake and Nolin River Lake, and some smallmouth are taken from Herrington Lake, Rough River Lake, Martins Fork Lake and Laurel River Lake.

The smallmouth is a terrific game fish—agile, strong and possessed with terrific endurance. His heart-stopping leaps and frantic, drag-screeching runs are amazing. Smallmouth seem to head for the surface as soon as they're hooked and jump repeatedly. The smallmouth's cover preferences are somewhat like those of the spotted bass. Submerged ledges, shallow gravel flats and steep banks that are next to the old river channel seem always to hold smallmouth.

The Kentucky Lake smallmouth bass fishery is worth discussing here since it is confined to just this kind of habitat. This fishery began to take off around 1977, when a few fish started showing up north of the Kentucky-Tennessee line. Prior to that time, smallmouth were routinely taken from the colder feeder streams in the Tennessee section of the impoundment. Fishing professional Ron Shearer of Hardin, who guides on the lake when he's not tournament fishing, said that he thinks the fishery "is on the verge of an explosion."

While smallmouths are being caught from the lake as far north as the dam, the rocky cliffs and points south of the US-68 bridge (Eggner Ferry Bridge) are consistently yielding bronzebacks in number. Clay Bay, Tischel Creek, Blue Springs, Panther Bay, Standing Rock Creek and

*Billy Westmorland with small-
mouth bass taken from Dale
Hollow Lake—courtesy of
Billy Westmorland*

virtually any embayment where a primary creek channel intersects the old river close to shore are prime smallmouth locations.

"I fish ¼-ounce jigs in black or brown (live rubber in warm weather and bucktail when the water's cold), dressed with Uncle Josh #101 pork spin frogs or U2 Twin Tails. Position the boat in deep water and cast into the shallower water, hopping the lure off the bottom," Shearer explained. Gravel bars in fifteen to twenty-five feet of water along the old river channels should also be worked deliberately and slowly.

Kentucky Lake is a shallower impoundment than traditional bronze-back haunts, highland reservoirs like Lake Cumberland or Dale Hollow Lake. "There's much more water color and reachable structure," Shearer said, adding that "light tackle will work here, but it's not necessary. I fish with a medium-action spinning rod and a reel spooled in 8-to-12-pound test line."

Shearer also suggests fishing for Kentucky Lake bronzebacks with crankbaits—the Reel Deep Wee-R, spinnerbaits (especially at night) and the Norman Deep Baby N. He recommends fishing creek channel ledges, the secondary points in embayments, long sloping rock points near the mouths of creeks, sand and gravel bars along the main river channel, and the creek channels themselves for suspended fish. Plastic worms, four- and six-inchers in amber, blood, blue and red firetails, motor oil, and electric grape augertails, as well as four-inch grubs, are effective on smallmouth.

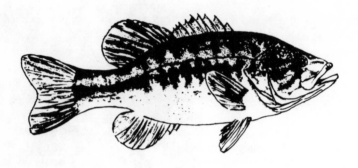

Spotted (Kentucky) Bass

The spotted bass has found a home in Kentucky and has endeared itself to anglers everywhere.

On February 27, 1956, Kentucky's General Assembly passed Senate Resolution 70 (joint resolutions have the power of law), establishing the spotted bass as Kentucky's official game fish. Soon afterwards, the legislation was signed into law by Governor Albert B. "Happy" Chandler.

From that date, this remarkable fish has been known as the "Kentucky bass," a common name that has apparently been accepted throughout much of the fish's geographic range.

The main reason why the spotted bass was made the namesake of the Commonwealth is because of its abundance in the Ohio River and the tributaries to the south. Somewhat of a regional fish, the spotted bass is found in streams of the Gulf Coast from Texas to the Florida panhandle, northward between the Appalachian divide and eastern Kansas to central Illinois, and the upper Ohio River Valley to southern Pennsylvania. In much of the northern United States the fish is known simply as a "spot."

Fishery biologists didn't recognize that the bass was a separate species until 1927, although many Ohio River commercial fishermen had known this long before then. Spotted bass usually don't grow to the size largemouth or smallmouth do. A spotted bass that weighs in excess of 4 pounds is something special; adults are commonly 8 to 15 inches in length, and 8 ounces to 2 pounds in weight. After reaching about 2¾ pounds, the spotted bass develops a very broad girth which tapers to a sleek, powerful forked tail.

The state record spotted bass was caught from a farm pond. It's believed that the fish was trapped in the pond by receding flood waters, where it grew to enormous size. The fish weighed 7 pounds, 10 ounces, and was caught by A. E. Sellers of Louisville on June 13, 1970, in Nelson County. The IGFA all-tackle world record spotted bass weighed 8 pounds, 15 ounces, and was caught from Lewis Smith Lake in Alabama by Philip C. Terry, Jr., on March 18, 1978.

Spotted bass are a cross between the largemouth and smallmouth in physical characteristics and habitat preferences, although they are not as widely distributed. Ichthyologists have taken spotted bass from every major river in Kentucky except for the Little Sandy. The fish seem to have adapted well to large impoundments and seem to be able to reproduce as well in lakes as in rivers.

A member of family Centrarchidae, the spotted bass, *Micropterus punctulatus*, has two major physical characteristics which separate it from the largemouth. The first is a small patch of teeth on the tongue, but the most prominent is the longitudinal rows of "dark spots" which form definite stripes on its pale belly. The spotted bass also has bright red eyes and an olive, diamond-studded back.

Spotted bass, much more than largemouths, school up, and are taken in "jumps." They are seldom loners. Catch one and chances are there's another close by. Spotted bass love crayfish and will feed on them whenever they can. Minnows, though, are their main food source. Sometimes they take large insects, but not often. They will also readily eat salamanders and nightcrawlers.

The types of structure that most often hold spotted bass are underwater humps or ridges next to the old river channel, steep bluffs, stair-stepped bluffs, long points, shelves and flats. Shadlike lures, four-inch plastic worms Texas rigged, jigs and grubs are top lure choices, although to fill the stringer consistently, you should fish with live bait. Wiggly, live creatures are without a doubt the ticket for big "hawg" spotted bass.

A peculiarity of spotted bass is their propensity to seek deep water. They almost invariably locate at depths deeper than other species of bass, often as deep as sixty feet or more if adequate amounts of dissolved oxygen are present, although underwater springs and current flow can oftentimes create water sufficiently oxygenated to support them at extreme depths. Big spotted bass are rarely caught at depths above fifteen feet.

Spotted bass are extremely strong for their size. They are very agile and leap well when hooked; many anglers feel that they even out-hustle the smallmouth. Spotted bass are found in all the lakes profiled in this book except Lake Malone, Dewey Lake and Greenbo Lake.

Spotted bass—photo by Soc Clay

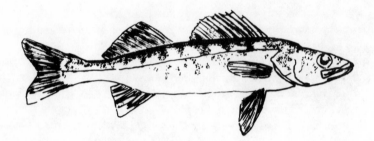

Walleye

The walleye is a member of the family Percidae, the perches and darters. Because of an intensive fishery-management effort, walleye are now thriving in many of the Kentucky lakes profiled in this book.

They are cold-water fishes that begin spawning runs in early spring and migrate to deep water during the summer months. The walleye has captured the attention of anglers because of a program in which "northern strain" fish, which have the ability to spawn in lakes on riprap and gravel flats, have been introduced into several Kentucky impoundments.

The walleye, *Stizostedion vitreum*, spawn when water temperatures reach 45 degrees. The fry eat crustaceans and insect larvae, but soon turn to small forage fish when they reach fingerling size.

Kentucky's state record walleye was taken from Lake Cumberland on October 1, 1958, by Abe Black, and the huge fish weighed 21 pounds, 8 ounces. The IGFA all-tackle world record walleye weighed 25 pounds, and was caught from Old Hickory Lake in Tennessee on August 1, 1960, by Mabry Harper. Kentucky's state record walleye is thought to be the third largest walleye ever caught in the States. The two other states that have produced trophy-size walleye in the 20-pound range are Arkansas and Missouri.

Kentucky's state record walleye was, of course, one of the so-called southern strain fish present in the Cumberland River prior to its impoundment. The fantastic walleye fishing in the headwaters of Lake Cumberland peaked in 1954 and gradually declined to the point that by 1966 the months of February and March were closed to walleye fishing in an effort to protect the spawning adults that remained.

The walleye fishing boom at Lake Cumberland was a phenomenon experienced in several states throughout the mid-South as large impoundments were built. The fish grow rapidly because of increased forage availability, but, unfortunately, southern strain walleye can't adapt reproductively to lake environments, and are eventually caught out by anglers.

Kentucky Department of Fish and Wildlife Resources predator fish biologist Benjy Kinman now manages the walleye program at Lake Cumberland. Between 1973 and 1977 12 million fingerlings were stocked.

Walleye—courtesy of
Kentucky Department of Fish
and Wildlife Resources

Kinman has been working for the past few years monitoring the progress of the northern strain walleye through considerable studying of the fish's food habits and reproduction.

The program has met with success, as adult fish are routinely caught from the lake or netted during population samplings. Spawning runs in Big South Fork of the Cumberland and headwater tributaries such as the Rockcastle River and Laurel River have been better in recent years, and the fishery is ripe for picking.

Laurel River Lake was initially stocked with walleyes. Barren River Lake is another major Kentucky lake where the walleye potential has been extensively studied and large stockings have been initiated. During a four-year period between 1973 and 1977, more than four million walleye fry were stocked in Barren River Lake. In 1977, 300,000 walleye fingerlings were stocked in Rough River Lake. Both lakes now have self-sustaining populations of walleye from the stockings.

The eggs and milt from northern strain adults captured in Lake Cumberland's headwater tributaries during the spring run are hatched at the Minor E. Clark Hatchery just below Cave Run Dam. The fry are raised in brooder ponds and stocked when they reach fingerling size.

Walleye fishing demands deep-water tactics, a thorough probing of submerged creek channels, underwater ridges and gravel points. Trolling bottom-bouncing crankbaits against the current, casting with jigs and doll flies and still-fishing with nightcrawlers and minnows are proven methods for catching walleyes. A sluggish fish, the walleye responds best to lures presented at a slow retrieve just off the bottom.

It's not real easy to tell the difference between a walleye and a sauger.

They look amazingly alike. But the walleye has a whitish lower lobe on the caudal fin and the sauger doesn't. The walleye also has a black spot on the basal portion of the pectoral fin and, internally, three pyloric caeca (fingerlike structures where the intestines leave the stomach), versus five to eight in the sauger.

Like the sauger, the walleye is a school fish, and excellent tablefare. The walleye has eyes that are super-sensitive to light, so they avoid sunlight. During the winter months walleye can be caught in surprisingly shallow water, whereas in the summer, they're usually in twenty to fifty feet of water, dissolved oxygen permitting.

In the Cumberland River, below Wolf Creek Dam, walleye can be caught in water from four to ten feet deep, since the discharge is from the bottom of the lake and is well within the walleye's preferred temperature range. The walleye in Lake Cumberland are as much of a neglected resource as the sauger in Kentucky Lake.

No other technique has revolutionized walleye fishing more than the Lindy Rig, perfected in the mid-1960s by Ron Lindner, with the help of his brother Al. This bottom-bouncing rig, developed in Minnesota, is devastating because it presents live bait as natural as possible. Mainly nightcrawlers or minnows are used, although leeches are a top bait up north.

The idea is to backtroll slowly and deliberately, bouncing the "walking sinker" across rocks and gravel flats, with the bait trailing on a floating jig head. Small crankbaits can also be used with the Lindy Rig. "Usually ⅜-ounce or heavier sinkers are used," explained Al Lindner, "depending on the depth to be fished, or the speed of the current [if you're fishing in a river, or tailwater, for example]."

The rig is made by first threading your line through the hole in the sinker and tying it to one end of a double swivel. Then tie an 18-inch piece of monofilament onto the other end of the swivel. The jig floats up off the bottom at a uniform depth. The slip sinker allows the angler to give the fish line for a brief run and time to swallow the bait before setting the hook.

The beauty of the Lindy Rig is that broad flats can be fished thoroughly and effectively. It was developed for use in the deep, rocky lakes of Minnesota, although it can be fished much easier in the shallow flats common in Kentucky's lakes and tailwaters.

The successful walleye angler is one who first locates fish-holding structure by carefully reading hydrographic maps, then probes these potential hotspots by fishing patiently and sticking with a game plan. Another rig that has been proven effective on walleyes is Dan Gapen's Bait Walker.

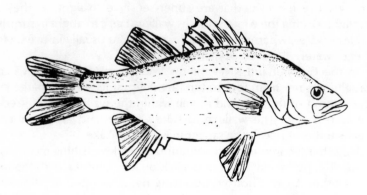

White Bass

The white bass is the most widely distributed of the three species of true basses, family Serranidae, found in Kentucky. This is predominantly a marine family, whose members are widely distributed in tropical and warm temperate seas; there are few true freshwater basses. The black basses (largemouth, spotted and smallmouth) aren't at all related to the white bass; they are actually members of the sunfish family, family Centrarchidae, and are "cousins" to the bluegill rather than the white bass.

Morone chrysops, the white bass, is found in all medium to large rivers in Kentucky and, consequently, in all of our impoundments over five thousand surface acres in size. They aren't found, however, in three small lakes profiled in this book—Lake Malone, Greenbo Lake and Martins Fork Lake. While most true basses are anadromous—that is, they spawn in fresh water and live in salt water—white bass stay in fresh water all their lives, migrating seasonally from small streams where they spawn in the spring to the large pools of rivers or lakes in the summer.

The white bass is a silvery rocket with fins. Constantly on the move, white bass school up by the hundreds. They are voracious feeders, so aggressive that the schools of shad they rip into will literally beach themselves if trapped against the bank. White bass are like finned wolves. Their run-and-gun feeding sprees, called "jumps," make the surface bubble and froth.

White bass in the two-to-three-pound class are magnificent fighters when taken on light tackle. They usually don't jump, but will make several deep runs. Kentucky's white bass record is held by two anglers, Lorne Eli and B. B. Hardin. Both fish weighed five pounds, and were taken from Kentucky Lake: Eli's on July 11, 1943, and Hardin's on June 3, 1957. The IGFA all-tackle world record white bass weighed five pounds, nine ounces, and was caught by David S. Cordill on March 31, 1977, from the Colorado River in Texas.

Although forage fishes make up the bulk of their diet, white bass will also feed on insects and crustaceans. To be successful at white bass fishing, anglers must capitalize on the seasonal movements of the fish. They are the earliest spawners on our warm-water game fish timetable. They begin to congregate when the water temperatures reach the upper 50s, their optimum spawning temperature being 60 degrees.

The old saying "The white bass run when the dogwoods are in bloom" has some substance to it, as the same kind of weather that brings out the blooms in these flowering trees also warms up the water enough to induce spawning. The correlation is phenomenal. White bass don't need current to spawn, but they prefer it to calm water, although curiously enough they are a pelagic species—that is, they live and feed in open water.

The headwater of Lake Cumberland, Rough River Lake, Nolin Lake and Barren River Lake have white bass runs each year. White bass are also taken in large numbers from the tailwaters below Kentucky Dam, Barkley Dam, Wolf Creek Dam (Lake Cumberland) and, to a lesser extent, all the dams of Kentucky's major impoundments. Declining white bass fisheries have plagued both Dewey Lake and Herrington Lake in recent years.

Spinners, surface poppers, shadlike crankbaits, spoons, do-jigs and live minnows are all tops for catching white bass. They really aren't that choosy. One rig which has been highly effective for years is the "plunker and fly" combination, said to have been perfected by white bass fishermen on Herrington Lake back in the 1930s.

A floating hookless plug with a popper lip (oftentimes a plunker is made by removing the hooks from a bass stick bait) gives the rig weight so it can be cast long distances. An 18-inch leader of 25-pound test monofilament is tied to the rear eyelet of the plug so that a jig or small spoon (anything flashy and white) can be trailed.

The plunker and fly rig is simply cast over a working jump and retrieved through it rapidly. The popping action of the plunker imitates a feeding white bass on the surface, the trailing fly a shad. The rig is sometimes effective if blind casted just after the school goes down. The heavy leader keeps the line from twisting. Long casts are generally the rule in white bass fishing because you never know where the fish are going to resurface.

In midsummer, after the jumps have ended, many anglers in Kentucky take white bass by trolling or night fishing over gas lanterns. Trolling with a white Bomber and a spoon trailing on a leader is highly productive, especially when schools are located by the use of a graph recorder or depth finder. Remove the rear hook of the Bomber and tie the leader to the eyelet on the nose of the lure.

A variety of spoons can be used. I have caught numerous white bass on the #1 Mepps with the green-jeweled finish. When flashing through the water, this spoon resembles a shad. I have also fished extensively with the Sidewinder spoon (copper finish) and Kastmaster, a spoon with a tuft of white hair wrapped on the treble hook. Stick baits, both floating and sinking ones like the Rebel or Striper Swiper, are effective on white bass in the jumps, as well as rockfish and rockfish–white bass hybrids. Crankbaits such as the Bagley's and Rebel Shad are also effective when trolled or cast into jumps.

Night fishing is a fun way to catch "silvers" during June, July and August. White bass are a popular summertime fish with houseboaters, who can relax while wetting a line from the deck. The bass are usually found in deep water, fifteen to thirty feet, off points and steep rock walls on the old river channel.

Gas lanterns can be attached to the sides of most boats easily with commercially available screw-on brackets. Be sure to get a reflector or use some aluminum foil to keep the light out of your eyes and pointed down into the water where it's supposed to be.

Automobile headlights, cradled in styrofoam and floating on top of the water, shine a brighter beam down into the water column than five lanterns ever will. About fifteen feet of lamp cord, alligator clips and a 12-volt battery are all that's needed to put you in business. I like to tape the end of the lamp cord with the headlight on it to a ten-foot section of cane pole, so that the beam can be positioned easier. Otherwise the light will float all around, and it's best to fish right down where the light is the brightest.

The strong light draws plankton, which in turn draws schools of shad. The white bass are not far behind. The trick in remembering the depth at which the fish are feeding is to lower your bait to the bottom and begin reeling it up slowly, counting the number of cranks of the reel handle off the bottom. When you start catching white bass, fish at that level.

When fishing the jumps or trolling in Lake Barkley and Kentucky Lake, it's not uncommon to catch the yellow bass, *Morone mississippi-ensis*, the white bass's cousin, which apparently is restricted to the Purchase region of Kentucky. Yellow bass are present in great numbers in the tailwaters of these twin impoundments and in the Ohio River lock and dam system. They have a yellowish coloration and a more slender head than the white bass, and they rarely reach two pounds.

Major Lakes of Kentucky

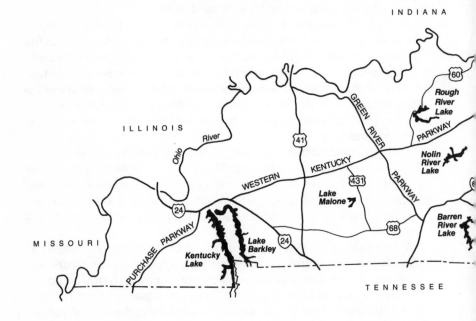

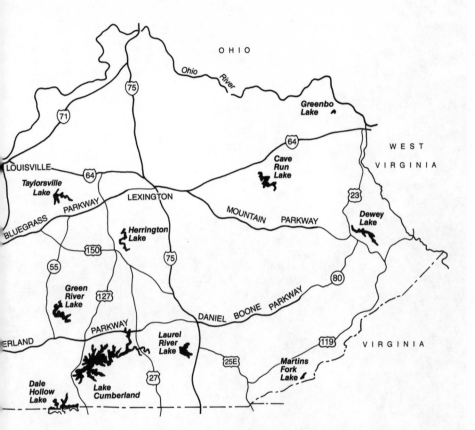

Photo by Soc Clay

The Lakes

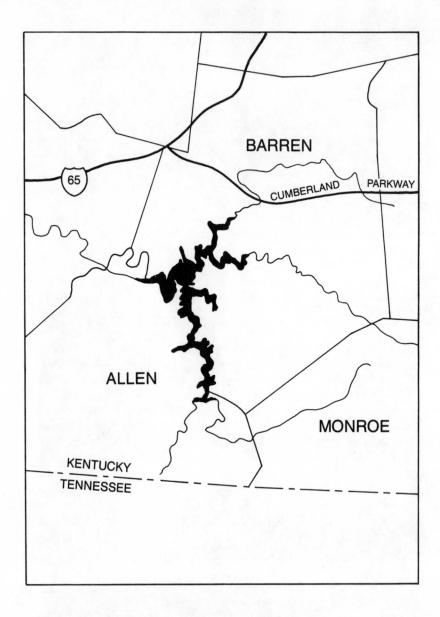

Barren River Lake

Location

Barren River Lake is approximately 103 miles south of Louisville in Barren, Monroe and Allen counties. The southernmost impoundment in the Louisville District of the U.S. Army Corps of Engineers, Barren River Lake is just 22 miles from the Kentucky-Tennessee border. The lake is accessible via highways Interstate-65, US-31E, Ky-1855, Ky-921, Ky-517, Ky-87, Ky-252 and Ky-98.

Completed in 1964, the lake was impounded from the Barren River, the largest tributary of the Green River. The U.S. Geological Survey topographic quadrangles in 1/24,000 scale for Barren River Lake are Austin, Fountain Run, Glasgow South, Holland, Lucas and Meador.

- No-Wake Embayments: None
- Outboard Motor Size Restrictions: None

Size

At summer pool, Barren River Lake has about 10,000 surface acres at elevation 552; the winter drawdown reduces the lake to 4,340 surface acres at elevation 525. The upper half of the lake is markedly affected by the winter pool level. The drawdown goes all the way to preimpoundment elevations of the old river channel, and miles of mud flats are exposed.

At its widest point, from Peninsula Recreation Area across Mason Island to the rock cliffs adjacent to Ky-252, Barren River Lake is approximately 7,920 feet wide. At summer pool, it has 140 miles of shoreline.

For more information write: Resource Manager, Barren River Lake, U.S. Army Corps of Engineers, Route 2, Box 184, Glasgow, KY 42141, or telephone (502) 646-2055.

Marinas

There are three marinas on Barren River Lake.

Walnut Creek Marina is 8 miles north of Scottsville off US-31E, via Ky-252 (.7 mile), then 2 miles east on Ky-1855. Open seasonally, the marina has a snack bar, artificial lures and tackles, live bait (shiner

minnows, nightcrawlers, red worms and carp dough) and gas (regular and mixed available). Both 14-foot fishing boats with 6.5-horsepower outboards and 15½- and 16½-foot bass boats, equipped with 65- and 75-horsepower outboards can be rented. A fish-cleaning station, freezer space and boat-launching ramp are also available. There are approximately 100 boat slips (75 covered and 25 open), plus numerous buoy tie-offs. For more information write: Walnut Creek Marina, Route 4, Box 200 C, Scottsville, KY 42164, or telephone (502) 622-5858.

The other two marinas on the lake are state-operated through concessionaires. Barren River Lake State Resort Park Dock, within walking distance of the park lodge, is open seasonally. There's a snack bar and gasoline sales (both regular and mixed available). There are 140 boat slips (100 open and 40 covered). Fourteen-foot aluminum boats with 7.5-horsepower outboards are available. Services for fishermen include bait and tackle sales and a fish-cleaning house nearby, with limited, free freezer space on the dock for guests. For more information write: Barren River Lake State Resort Park Dock, Lucas, KY 42156, or telephone (502) 646-2357.

The Peninsula Marina, on Ky-252, 2 miles north of the dam, is open twenty-four hours during holidays, 8:00 A.M. to 11:00 P.M. on weekdays,

Barren River Lake State Resort Park—courtesy of Kentucky Department of Public Information

and 7:00 A.M. to 11:00 P.M. weekends. There are 100 covered boat slips, plus a snack bar and live bait. Rental boats include 14-foot johnboats with 6-horsepower outboards, 24-foot pontoon boats and 42- and 45-foot houseboats. For more information write: Peninsula Marina, Route 2, Glasgow, KY 42141, or telephone (502) 646-2223.

Fishing

While the largemouth bass usually gets the lion's share of attention in outdoor magazines and newspaper columns, it's no secret that Barren River Lake offers good fishing for other species too—crappie, rockfish–whitebass hybrids and catfish (flatheads, blue cats and channels).

If you don't think so, just ask Allen County conservation officer John Sawyers. He says that the upper end of the lake (above the US-31E bridge) offers some good catfish fishing during the hot dog days. "In the summer months I check the fishing licenses of hundreds of anglers who drive from as far away as Louisville and Lexington, just to go after those big cats," he said. And just how big do catfish get in Barren River Lake? Sawyers said that the largest flathead he's aware of that's been taken from the lake was a fifty-pounder. "There are also a great many good-sized channels, blues and yellow cats in the lake," Sawyers added.

Recent data substantiate this claim. A 2.96-acre population study during the summer of 1982 yielded ninety-two harvestable channel cats, many of which were in the three-to-four-pound class and about twenty-one inches in length. "The shallow flats adjacent to the submerged river channel are ideal for trotlines, juggin' and fishing from the bank," Sawyers said. Shad cut bait, stink and blood baits and large shiners are recommended for enticing those big fellas to bite.

The crappie is also a popular fish with weekend anglers and families. Humpbacks and stump beds along submerged creek channels offer the best cover for schools of crappie in the summer and winter. The flatland reservoir isn't difficult to fish, and most times crappie can be found in eight to fifteen feet of water. Beaver Creek, Skaggs Creek, Peter Creek and Walnut Creek are good crappie fishing embayments.

"Barren is the kind of lake where you can almost always catch a mess of fish, if you don't care what kind of fish you're going after. The white bass and crappie fishing is excellent at times, and there's no doubt that Barren is one of our top bass fishing lakes," explained Ted Crowell, assistant director of fisheries for the Kentucky Department of Fish and Wildlife Resources.

Crappie—photo by author

While working as the department's bass biologist, Crowell conducted a mark and recapture (tagging) study, as well as age and growth research on Barren River Lake. What he found was that bass in Barren exhibit average growth rates and reproductive potential, with good year-class recruitment. "The exploitation rate for twelve-inch and longer bass [keepers] was relatively low, about 27 percent, and there appears to be an expanding smallmouth bass population."

Improving smallmouth bass fishing in the so-called warm-water impoundments is something that's occurring in several Kentucky man-made lakes—most notably Kentucky Lake and Green River Lake. The reason? "It's all speculative, but honestly I think it's cyclic. The reason may revolve around the big shad die-off during the severe winter of 1977–78," Crowell said. "While the loss of shad forage hurt the large-mouth, it didn't affect the smallmouth. Their reproduction rate was the same, but they gained percentagewise in the overall population. Also, there was not as intense competition for food with the largemouths.

"Now these fish of the 1978 year-class are spawning adults, and there is some speculation that they may carry the trend," Crowell said. Biologists believe that another reason for the expansion of smallmouth bass in our large impoundments, especially Kentucky Lake, is wave action, annual pool fluctuations and river channel current, which each year pushes more silt and mud downstream, exposing rock shelves and gravel beds. The smallmouth's preferred food is crayfish, and this habitat change directly benefits this crustacean. As its food source expands, the smallmouth becomes more firmly established—and more visible in the fisherman's creel.

The smallmouth tend to remain on the shale bluffs and gradually sloping gravel points on the lower end of Barren River Lake. The large-mouth, on the other hand, seem to migrate seasonally in the impoundment. The upper end of the lake produces best in the early spring and in the late fall prior to the drawdown in early September. During the summer and throughout the winter, the lower end of the impoundment offers the best fishing.

Some anglers believe that during the summer many largemouths suspend in the submerged channels of the larger tributaries or the old river channel in deep water that can be reached only by trolling crankbaits or vertical jigging spoons or by working adjacent structure with a plastic worm. Donald Depp, the Barren County conservation officer, explained that there's considerable interest in fishing deep structure because that's where bigger fish are usually caught.

Cecil Gorley calls the deep-water lure used by local anglers the "Barren River Rig." Depp said, "It's a six-inch purple firetail plastic worm

Guide Harlyn Nall with crappie from a few hours of fishing over deep-water structure in March—photo by author

rigged on a ⅛-to-⅜-ounce jig made locally by Bobby Wade. The rig is fished almost vertically and bounced off drops and stair-step ledges; the strike usually comes when the lure is falling."

"Model-A Bombers in chartreuse and crayfish patterns are especially effective," Sawyers explained, adding that a productive pattern on Barren River Lake in the summertime is fishing these crankbaits over deep points.

Gerry Buynak, bass biologist for Kentucky's Division of Fisheries, rates Barren River Lake as one of Kentucky's top largemouth lakes. While collecting reproductive and standing crop data during studies in August 1982, Buynak found that there were about nine legal bass per acre in the study areas, with an estimate of 852 pounds per acre in Barren River Lake. "The lake has a heavy shad population, and bass taken during the sampling ranged up to 6.02 pounds, and about twenty-one inches in length," Buynak said.

During a spring electrofishing sample seven keeper bass were taken from the riprap along the US-31E bridge. "It's a fine bass lake, one of our best. It and Herrington were the tops we sampled this summer [1982]," Buynak went on. Southwest District fishery biologist Bonny Dale Laflin, however, cautioned that "fishing pressure is phenomenal, and the average size of largemouth in the lake is smaller than in previous years."

Depp said that he has also noted some changes in the impoundment. "Silting isn't a major problem, but I have noticed in the last five years that there's been a shift from fescue to row crops in the lake's watershed. This change in farming practices has caused some of the creek channels to fill in ever so slightly."

Another fish that's drawing considerable attention is the rockfish–white bass hybrid. "In May of 1982 we stocked about 200,000 of them in Barren; they're coming from Florida," Crowell explained, adding, "We traded walleye fingerlings for them." Hybrids were previously stocked in 1979 and 1981, after stockings of purebred rockfish in the early and middle 1970s failed to establish a fishery. "There are a few of the purebreds left, but not many," Depp said. During population samplings in the fall of 1982, two distinct sizes of rockfish-white bass hybrids were taken in gill nets. "We had fish between 5.3 inches and 7.0 inches in one year-class [1981] and 19 inches to 21 inches in the other [1979]," Laflin reported, adding that "the two year-classes stocked seem to be well established."

The white bass has always been well established in Barren River Lake. Fish of six to eight inches in length are common. During the summer of 1982, cove population studies yielded more than 500 white bass and hybrids from the Peter Creek embayment near Barren River Lake State Resort Park.

The headwaters of the lake, roughly above the mouth of Walnut Creek, hold white bass in the springtime during their run. Do-jigs, Little George, Mepps spoons and small spinners in white, yellow or shad color are excellent prespawn lures. They also can be effectively used later in the year when the white bass congregate in the main lake to chase schools of shad. The 31E bridge, at the mouth of Hurricane Creek, is an excellent area of the lake to fish in early summer, especially at night with minnows over a gas lantern.

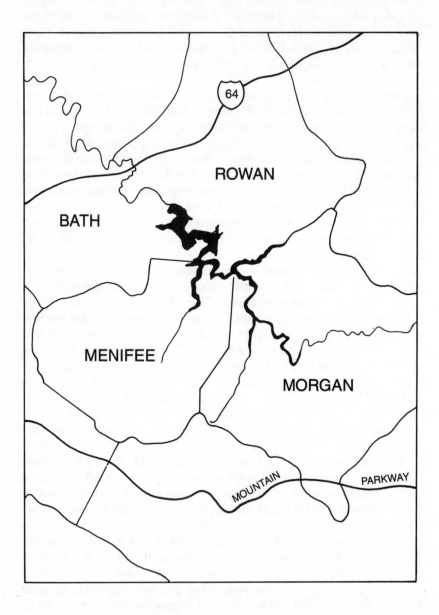

ROWAN

BATH

MENIFEE

MORGAN

MOUNTAIN   PARKWAY

Cave Run Lake

Location

Cave Run Lake is approximately 60 miles east of Lexington, just a few minutes drive from Morehead. The impoundment is totally within the northernmost ranger district of Daniel Boone National Forest, covering parts of Menifee, Morgan, Bath and Rowan counties.

The lake is best reached from the west via Interstate-64 and US-60. Other highways which provide access are Ky-801, Ky-826, Ky-772, Ky-519, Ky-211 and Ky-1274; three U.S. Forest Service gravel roads lead to recreational areas surrounding the lake—FS road 918, 1017 and 129.

The lake, and the rugged forestlands of the Cumberland Plateau which provide a scenic backdrop, can be found on the following U.S. Geological Survey topographic quadrangles in 1/24,000 scale: Farmers, Salt Lick, Colfax, Morehead, Bangor, Ezel, West Liberty, Wrigley and Lenox.

- No-Wake Embayments: None
- Outboard Motor Size Restrictions: None

Size

Cave Run Lake was built under the authority of the Louisville District of the U.S. Army Corps of Engineers. Construction on the impoundment began in May 1965; the project was completed February 8, 1974. The damsite is 173.6 miles above the mouth of the Licking River, which empties into the Ohio River at Covington.

At summer pool, 48.1-mile-long Cave Run Lake has about 8,270 surface acres at elevation 730 feet; the winter drawdown reduces the lake to 7,390 surface acres at elevation 724. Cave Run Lake has 166 miles of shoreline at summer pool.

Total storage capacity of the impoundment is 14,870 surface acres, and the drainage area above the dam is 826 square miles. The cost of the project was $83 million.

For more information write: Resource Manager, U.S. Army Corps of Engineers, Cave Run Lake, Route 4, Box 223, Morehead, KY 40351, or telephone (606) 784-9709.

Marinas

There are two marinas on Cave Run Lake, both operating on federally owned land through a lease agreement with the U.S. Forest Service.

Scott Creek Marina is the largest marina on the lake. Located just above the dam, near the mouth of Scott Creek, the marina is 2 miles east of Farmers off Ky-801. Open year-round, sixteen hours a day, the marina has a grocery store and a restaurant, which is open sixteen hours a day in season and twelve hours a day on Saturdays and Sundays only during the off-season. There are 200 boat slips, 92 of which are covered. Live bait (minnows and nightcrawlers), an excellent assortment of bass and muskellunge lures and boating supplies are available. Cushions and life preservers are provided when you rent a 14-foot aluminum fishing boat with 9.9-horsepower outboard.

In addition, the 24-foot pontoon boats, bass boats and 45- and 50-foot houseboats are available. The 50-footers sleep as many as ten. For more information on either Scott Creek Marina or Longbow Marina write: Cave Run Marinas, Box 174, Morehead, KY 40351, or telephone (606) 784-9666.

The satellite marina at Longbow, 5 miles north of Frenchburg, off Ky-1274, is owned by the same concessionaire as the Scott Creek Marina. Longbow has 60 boat slips (44 covered), 14-foot fishing boats (rental price the same as at Scott Creek Marina) and grocery, live bait and tackle sales. Both marinas have boat-launching ramps nearby. Longbow Marina is open seasonally, April to mid-November, 6:00 A.M. to 10:00 P.M.. The telephone number at Longbow is (606) 768-2929.

Fishing

Even before the Licking River was impounded, creating Cave Run Lake, anglers were harvesting silver muskies with regularity from Kentucky's fifth largest river, which drains 3,670 square miles. Given the muskie-producing ability of the river system, it's not surprising that a man-made impoundment was created that rivals even the most productive muskie lakes of the north country.

The extensive stockings of fingerlings in the mid-1970s, all raised at the newly opened Minor E. Clark Hatchery, helped expand the fisheries to a level that has far surpassed the river's potential before impoundment. "Formation of the lake set the stage for the emergence of a major muskie fishery unrivaled anywhere else in Kentucky," explained Lou Kornman, Northeast District fishery biologist for the Kentucky Department of Fish and Wildlife Resources.

Between 1974 and 1980, according to department records, 63,761 fingerlings ranging in size from four to nine inches were stocked in the lake. Of that total, almost 40 percent were eight-to-nine-inch fish stocked in 1979 and 1980. Fish stocked in 1981 and 1982 were even bigger, some twelve to fourteen inches.

A study released in 1980 by fishery biologist Jim Axon, "Development of the Muskellunge Fishery in Cave Run Lake," indicated that for the first few years after impoundment, it took muskies less than three years to reach the legal harvest size of thirty inches. However, competition, food availability and other factors that influence the population dynamics of all man-made lakes have contributed to a slower, but still healthy, growth rate for the big fish in recent years.

Kornman said that the average size of legal muskies taken from Cave Run Lake in 1979 was about thirty-five inches, and the varying lengths of some keepers caught recently reinforce the theory that the massive stockings are paying off, as the lake has developed strong year-classes, easily recognizable by the lengths and weights of samples taken. On April 2, 1982, a muskie that weighed more than forty-one pounds, less than two pounds off the state record, was harvested.

There also were scattered reports of muskies caught that were smaller than the size stocked, which would indicate that reproduction is occurring. The question whether natural reproduction is occurring in streams which feed into the lake, however, hasn't been answered satisfactorily, according to Korman. "We've observed mature pairs in the shallows during the spring spawn, and have actually shocked up, tagged and released females full of eggs, but we've never captured any fry," he said.

"In the spring of 1978, Axon tagged sixty-one adults in shallow-water spawning sites. "I'd say without a doubt that muskies are spawning in the feeder streams of Cave Run Lake, but it's the stockings that are keeping the population up," Axon explained.

Sections of the lake that have proven productive include Beaver Creek, both Little and Big Cave Run creeks, Caney Creek, Leatherwood Creek, Fugate Hollow, Ramey Creek, Blackwater Creek and the Licking River at the lake's headwaters. Muskie have been caught from virtually every embayment of the lake, as well as from the small coves off the main lake within sight of the dam.

The best fishing weather is drizzly, overcast days. In the fall, those first few days when cold fronts hit are especially good. The muskie fishing usually picks up in August, from the period of inactivity that follows the spawn. The muskie usually go to deep water when hot weather hits, suspending off channel droplines or flooded treetops. Fish the primary points where shallow water is adjacent to the old river channel during late spring and early summer.

It seems that more fish are taken in the autumn than in the spring, although the real whoppers are usually harvested in February, March and April. In springtime, fish the heads of embayments in extremely shallow water. Never pass up a flooded cedar treetop. Giant muskie lures popular in the north country, like the Creeper, Hawg Wobbler, Splashtail, bucktails, and Daredevil spoon, are ideal for shallow-water fishing, when it's important to draw attention and to try to intimidate muskie into striking. The importance of figure-eighting your lure at the boat can't be stressed enough. Many follow-ups turn into strikes.

Local expert, and part-time guide at Cave Run Lake, Joe Smoot can attest to the difficulty of landing big muskellunges in Cave Run Lake's heavy cover. "They'll powerdive on you. If you can't turn 'em, you can bet there will be a flooded treetop nearby that they'll get tangled up in," Smoot explained. Since the lake was impounded, Smoot has boated over twenty keepers and has had some running battles with giant fish whose acrobatics and strength have been phenomenal, even for a veteran like Smoot.

"I've had muskies snap number-05 hooks, come blasting out of the water like a Polaris missile, or head to the deep six, snapping thirty-pound test monofilament with ease. I know I hooked one fish three different times and never got close to landing him," Smoot related.

In the spring, many anglers use smaller lures, especially Model-A Bombers. Buzzbaits in chartreuse, like the Lunker Lure, or exotic surface frothers, like the Timber Buzz, Floyd's Buzzer, Cry Baby and Blakemore Twister, have been used with much success by anglers at Cave Run Lake. "When I buy a buzzbait, I tie it to my truck antenna for a few days. Those baits really don't squeak right until they're just about worn out," Smoot said.

Trolling enthusiasts seem to prefer the timber-lined channel of Beaver Creek and the rocky humpbacks in the lower third of the lake. Many big fish are taken from this structure. The flooded timber in Caney Creek is a crankbait fisherman's dream come true. Lots of muskie are taken on 900 series Hellbenders (white, glitter finish) and big Bagley crankbaits. Giant Mister Twister spinnerbaits are effective when fished in the scattered weed beds found in small coves in the lower end of the lake.

The largemouth and spotted (Kentucky) bass are the most sought after game fish after the muskie. The Zilpo Flats, just across the lake from the mouth of Big Cave Run Creek, are a prime spot for casting crankbaits and working plastic worms through stumps or brush piles. The flats lie in about ten feet of water just off the main channel, which is in about forty feet of water.

There are submerged rock piles, old roadbeds, ponds and stump rows. The flats are quite large, and it would take days to work the entire area. During the winter drawdown there's a navigational buoy in the center of the flats, where a huge humpback is visible.

The south bank of Caney Creek is also a bass hotspot. There are shallow timbered flats, submerged creek channels and submerged tree-tops. The headwaters of Scott Creek next to the giant Canada goose rearing area is also an excellent spot for largemouths, with its flooded grasses, stumps and submerged creek channel. Early in the morning and late in the afternoon in the spring and fall, or at night in the summer, this area is ideal for fishing surface lures. My favorites for this area of the lake are the Boy Howdy, Rapala and Devil's Horse.

Cave Run Lake also offers some excellent crappie fishing. Cover is abundant, especially flooded timber and brush piles, and the forage availability must be good because studies have shown that the numbers of crappie and pounds per acre of crappie have increased dramatically since 1975. For example, the number of crappie per acre in 1975 was estimated at 1.2; the 1979 figure was 8.0 crappie per acre.

Part of this impressive gain can no doubt be attributed to the expanding fishery of a new lake, but this increase in numbers was accompanied by no drop-off in size. Although it hasn't been documented, I suspect that predation by muskies may be partly responsible for this success. Reducing the numbers always benefits crappie size.

The traditional crappie techniques of fishing with jigs in brush piles and the treetops of flooded standing timber, drifting minnows across stump rows and brush piles along the edges of submerged creek channels and dipping minnows in shoreline cover in the spring work fine in Cave Run Lake. There are extensive stump beds in Scott Creek, the Zilpo Flats and on the west bank of the main lake across from the Twin Knobs Campground. These are top areas of the lake for deep-water crappie fishing prior to and after the spawning run.

The Leatherwood Branch of Beaver Creek is also a top crappie embayment. Work the creek channel all the way to its mouth. Crappie are usually taken at the intersection of the channel with an old roadbed or in sections where standing timber hugs the channel dropline. Sassy Shad, Curlytails, the weedless Slider Head jigs, fuzzy grubs, do-jigs and the Roadrunner all work fine, but just about any lead-headed jig will do.

I find that white, pink and yellow are the most productive colors, not only in Cave Run Lake but in most any of Kentucky's major lakes. To give them added appeal, I usually hook a minnow (up from the lower jaw through the snout) on all my jigs, except those which have built-in tail-wiggling action, such as the Sassy Shad.

Cave Run Dam and Minor E. Clark Hatchery—courtesy of U.S. Army Corps of Engineers

Spotted (Kentucky) bass are also abundant in Cave Run Lake. Fish the upper part of the lake in the vicinity of the Ky-1274 bridge and the lower stretches of the old river channel where it hugs rocky, steep banks. One particularly productive spot on the lower end is just above the dam, at the junction of Scott Creek and the old river channel. The two submerged channels meet just off the bank in about twenty feet of water. Also, fish the riprap along the face of the dam and the submerged roadbed that runs the length of the bank from the mouth of Scott Creek to the dam. White jigs rigged with white pork split tails and ¼-ounce white spinnerbaits are top spotted bass lures.

Day in and day out, spotted bass are a lot easier to locate in the lake than largemouths. Sections of the bank which have numerous rock ledges or gravel points always hold spotted bass. I have a feeling that many largemouths suspend in or around the old river channel or in the treetops of flooded standing timber in fifteen to twenty-five feet of water when warm weather hits, because the times I have fished for largemouths in Cave Run Lake in the summer, they certainly weren't on the banks.

I've never tried vertical jigging spoons for largemouth bass in this lake before, but it should work in flooded timber adjacent to the old river channel. The optimum line test for bass fishing in the lake is 14-pound; 10-pound when the water clears. The number-one largemouth bass lure on the lake is the plastic worm. Motor oil, black and purple are top colors.

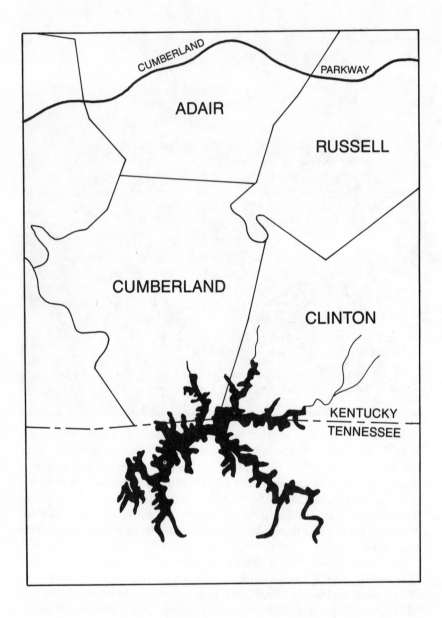

Dale Hollow Lake

Location

Dale Hollow Lake is approximately 132 miles south of Lexington in Cumberland and Clinton counties of Kentucky and Clay, Overton, Pickett and Fentress counties of Tennessee. Completed in 1943, Dale Hollow was one of the first impoundments built by the U.S. Army Corps of Engineers under the Flood Control Act of 1938.

The Kentucky portion of Dale Hollow Lake is accessible via several highways—Cumberland Parkway, Ky-90, Ky-61, US-127, Ky-485, Ky-449, Ky-1206, Ky-1351, Ky-553, Ky-738 and Tn-53. Dale Hollow Lake was built under the authority of the Nashville, Tennessee, District of the U.S. Army Corps of Engineers, and controls the runoff from a drainage area of 935 square miles.

The U.S. Geological Survey topographic quadrangles in 1/24,000 scale for the lake are Albany, Blacks Ferry, Byrdstown, Dale Hollow Dam, Dale Hollow Reservoir, Frogue and Moodyville.

- No-Wake Embayments: None
- Outboard Motor Size Restrictions: None

Size

Impounded from the Obey River, Dale Hollow Lake is southwest of Albany, straddling the Kentucky-Tennessee border. The rocky, cool lake is 160 feet deep at the lower end, just above the dam. The largest city close to the damsite is Celina, Tennessee. Sulphur Creek, Illwill Creek, Fanny's Creek and Wolf River are the major embayments in the Kentucky portion of the lake.

Most of the 61-mile-long lake is in Tennessee. At summer pool, Dale Hollow Lake has about 27,700 surface acres at elevation 651; the winter drawdown reduces the lake to 21,880 surface acres at elevation 631. At flood-control pool, 30,990 surface acres at elevation 663, there are about 620 miles of shoreline.

Kentucky's oldest man-made impoundment over 5,000 surface acres in size, Dale Hollow Lake is one of the state's most beautiful. Many of the secluded coves are spring-fed, and the water is gin clear. Towering beech, oak, maple and evergreen trees grow right to the water's edge. On the

Dale Hollow Lake—photo by Soc Clay

main lake, the backdrop is rolling, forested hills and rocky shoreline.

For more information write: Resource Manager, Dale Hollow Lake, U.S. Army Corps of Engineers, Route 1, Celina, TN 38551, or telephone (615) 243-3136.

Marinas

There are five marinas on the Kentucky portion of Dale Hollow Lake— Hendrick's Creek Resort, Sulphur Creek Marina, Wisdom Fishing Camp, Wolf River Dock, and Dale Hollow Lake State Park Marina.

Hendrick's Creek Resort is 11 miles south of Burkesville off Ky-61. Open mid-March through October, the dock has 35 boat slips, 20 covered. A boat-launching ramp, tackle and live bait—minnows, night-crawlers, red worms and meal worms—are available. Fishing boats, 14- and 16-footers, can be rented, either with or without the 6-to-20-horse-power outboards. Both electric and manual start models are available; security deposits are required. Houseboats are also available. For more information write: Hendrick's Creek Resort, Route 4, Burkesville, KY 42717, or telephone (502) 433-7172.

Sulphur Creek Marina is 6.5 miles south of Burkesville on Ky-61, then 2.5 miles south on Ky-485. The marina is open seasonally, April 1 to

October 31, and is equipped for mixed and regular gas sales and tackle and bait sales—crickets, minnows and nightcrawlers. There are 75 boat slips, 25 covered and 50 open; a restaurant and grocery are open seasonally. Rental boats include both 15-foot fishing boats, equipped with 7.5-to-15-horsepower outboards, and houseboats. Off-season rates are available. For more information write: Sulphur Creek Marina, Star Route 4, Box 39, Kettle, KY 45752, or telephone (502) 433-7272.

Wisdom Fishing Camp is approximately 5 miles west of Albany on Ky-553. Open year-round, the marina has 40 covered slips, 20 open; there's a fish-cleaning station and freezer space available. The restaurant is open from early May through mid-October. Other facilities and services include a boat-launching ramp, live bait (minnows and nightcrawlers), tackle and artificial lures, propane gas, mechanic on duty, regular and mixed gas. Fishing boats, aluminum 14-footers with 6-to-25-horsepower outboards, and houseboats can be rented. The houseboats feature propane grills. For more information write: Wisdom Fishing Camp, Route 2, Albany, KY 42602, or telephone (606) 387-5821.

Wolf River Dock is approximately 6 miles south of Albany on Ky-738. Open April 1 to November 1, the marina has 80 boat slips, all covered. The 14-foot fishing boats can be rented either with or without the 7.5-to-25-horsepower outboards. Other services and facilities include launching ramp, regular gas, fishing tackle and boating supplies, live bait (worms, minnows and crickets), fish-cleaning station and freezer space for guests. The rental 23-foot pontoon boats come with 35- and 50-horsepower outboards. For more information write: Wolf River Dock, Route 2, Box 172, Albany, KY 42602, or telephone (606) 387-5841.

Dale Hollow Lake State Park Marina is at Frogue, 12 miles south of Burkesville, and is reached via Ky-61, Ky-449, and Ky-1206. Open April 1 to October 31, the dock has 37 double open boat slips, a fish-cleaning station, a 75-foot by 220-foot concrete boat-launching ramp, regular and mixed gas sales. Tackle and live bait—minnows and red worms—are available. The restaurant is open Memorial Day to Labor Day. Both 14-foot fishing boats with 10-horsepower outboards and 20-foot pontoon boats with 35-horsepower outboards are available. For more information write: Dale Hollow Lake State Park Marina, Bow, KY 42714, or telephone (502) 433-7490.

Fishing

Dale Hollow Lake has gained a strong regional reputation and somewhat of a national following among anglers because of its fabulous smallmouth bass fishery.

On July 11, 1955, David Hayes of Leitchfield was trolling a bomber near the confluence of Illwill Creek and the Wolf River embayment when a lunker smallmouth struck. But what Hayes boated was not your typical braggin'-size smallmouth that tips the scales at 6 or 7 pounds. The fish weighed 11 pounds, 15 ounces, and established not only a new Kentucky state record but an IGFA all-tackle world record as well.

More than twenty-three years later a second Kentucky state record game fish—a 43-pound silver muskie caught on March 13, 1978, by Poter Hash, of Edmonton—was taken from Dale Hollow Lake. I think it's ironic that this impoundment, which has yielded two state record fish, isn't even managed by our own Department of Fish and Wildlife Resources. Dale Hollow Lake's fisheries are managed by biologists of the Tennessee Wildlife Resource Agency (TWRA), since only about 8 percent of the surface acreage is actually in Kentucky.

Records aside, the impoundment continues to offer quality fishing, albeit difficult fishing, during most of the year—especially the traditional vacation period from June through September. I think that one reason why the fishing has continued to be excellent at this time (forty years) is that it's a tough impoundment to learn, and not everybody catches fish, much less limits. There's plenty of fishing pressure, but not much angler success. You've got to be determined and fish hard if you expect to beat this lake; but the successful anglers will tell you it's worth the effort. Tried-and-true techniques developed over the years are the ticket to success on Dale Hollow Lake.

Fine strings of white bass, largemouth bass, spotted bass, walleye and rainbow trout are taken from Dale Hollow Lake each year with little fanfare and hoopla, compared to the attention focused on those giant muskies and the limits of chunky "brown" bass. Through a reciprocal agreement, both Kentucky and Tennessee fishing licenses are honored in the clearly marked sections of Wolf River embayment and Illwill Creek along the Kentucky-Tennessee border.

Billy Westmorland of Celina, Tennessee, one of the top smallmouth fishermen anywhere, has chased bronzebacks for over thirty years. Westmorland authored the classic book *Them Ol' Brown Fish* and has caught hundreds of smallmouth that would be considered trophy fish. His largest to date was a 10-pound, 1-ounce lunker taken on March 17, 1972, with a jig and pork rind leech combination. Westmorland considers the "pig and jig" combination tops for Dale Hollow Lake smallmouth.

Westmorland stresses using light tackle—spiderweb thin line (four-, six- and eight-pound test monofilament) and sensitive graphite rods. The pig and jig combination is favored over all other lures year-round, although in early spring floating minnow stick baits and crankbaits are also fished.

The ⅛-to-⅜-ounce jigs should be rigged with a pork rind eel or leech that is less than 2¾ inches long. "I have found that the style of pork trailer isn't nearly as important as the size," said Westmorland. "I prefer the Uncle Josh pork rinds; E2 and U2 are my favorite sizes." Westmorland also uses the ½-ounce Pedigo Spinnrite with a maribou tail, and fishes it slow along the bottom.

His favorite technique for fishing the jig and pork rind combination is "swimming." Some oldtimers call this method the "do nothing" because the lure is simply cast out and allowed to sink on a tight line toward the boat. The trick is for the rig to "float" down the water column. Another technique is the "free fall" to the bottom. He uses a heavier jig for this method, ¼ to ⅜ ounces. As soon as the lure hits, it is jerked off the bottom and bounced along off rock shelves and gravel. If the bouncing isn't fruitful, he sometimes twitches the jig to give it more action.

Westmorland's favorite jigs are the Hess Fly, Dragon Fly, Doll Fly, Sliders and Whirley Bees, as well as quality homemade jigs in brown and black. From late February–early March through April, Westmorland suggests fishing "the back ends of embayments, where the water warms up first. I fish minnowlike surface lures such as the A.C. Shiner, Rapala, and Bagley Bang-a-Lure."

Westmorland fishes crankbaits for most of March. "Slice the points from every angle with long casts. Those flat points with wide contours are the smallmouth spawning grounds," he explained, adding that "stained water is preferred. The next best situation is overcast days, with windy, choppy conditions. Fish the points where the chop is moving into the banks."

Along the Kentucky-Tennessee border, from west to east, Westmorland recommends fishing for smallmouth bass in the headwaters of Poor Branch, Natty Branch, Pusley Creek, Williams Branch of Sulphur Creek, the headwaters of Fanny's Creek, Hogback Creek of Illwill Creek and Spring Creek of the Wolf River embayment in the early spring. The Spring Creek section is also a top spot for white bass, as is Casey Branch of Sulphur Creek.

Late April through May is also a good time to catch largemouth. Westmorland suggests fishing stands of willow trees at the back ends of embayments. "I rig the worm without a weight and retrieve it with short, erratic jerks," he explained. The Sweet Willie, Ding-a-Ling and Sportsman Floater are some brands of plastic worms Westmorland uses.

Other cold-water fishes of considerable importance in Dale Hollow Lake are the walleye, lake trout, rainbow trout and silver muskie. The two-story fishery is remarkable indeed because of its quality. I know of no other lake in Kentucky that suggests so many different species of fish coexisting with so much growth potential.

The presence of lake trout (*Salvelinus namaycush*) in Dale Hollow Lake is a perfect example of what imaginative fishery management combined with a quality environment can produce. This deep-water fish, generally associated with the St. Lawrence, Hudson and drainages of the Great Lakes and western Canada, was quietly introduced into Dale Hollow Lake in 1975.

In the late 1970s, a few of them began showing up in fishermen's creels, and in the summer of 1982 the third class of lake trout was placed in the lake. "About one-half million have been stocked since the beginning of the project. This year's [1982] stocking class were three-to-four-inch fish," explains Anders Myhr, a fishery biologist with the TWRA working out of Jackson, Tennessee. The first group of lake trout stocked in Dale Hollow were raised at the federal fish hatchery on the Obey River.

Myhr said that anglers trolling with downriggers just above the dam have reported catching lake trout in the five-to-nine-pound range. To create a more stable forage base for the lake trout and other species, alewives have been placed in the lake, since the cold winter weather causes massive die-offs of threadfin shad.

Since the 1960s rainbow trout have also been stocked in Dale Hollow Lake at the rate of about 60,000 a year. During trout season, between May and November, the fish are taken primarily by deep trolling or fishing in twenty-five to fifty feet of water with nightcrawlers at night by the light of gas lanterns.

The muskie is another case in point for Dale Hollow's amazing productivity. There aren't as many of these big predators in Dale Hollow Lake as compared to Cave Run Lake, for example, but the average size is considerably more. The population is maintaining itself through natural reproduction, since there's no stocking. There are some whoppers, in the truest sense of the word, lurking in Dale Hollow Lake; some muskie die-hards believe that a world record "briartooth" will someday be caught from the impoundment.

The section of the lake between Irons Creek and the junction of the Wolf River embayment consistently produces big muskies. The best fishing method is trolling huge crankbaits during the winter months, especially January through March, on twenty-to-twenty-five-foot contours. Weed beds are a key to muskie success, and they are plentiful around Trooper Island and Horse Island. Other recommended sections of the lake for muskie fishing are Poor Branch, the old river channel between Hendricks Creek and Pusley Creek, and the primary point at the mouth of Moore Branch and Sulphur Creek.

Dale Hollow Lake—photo by Soc Clay

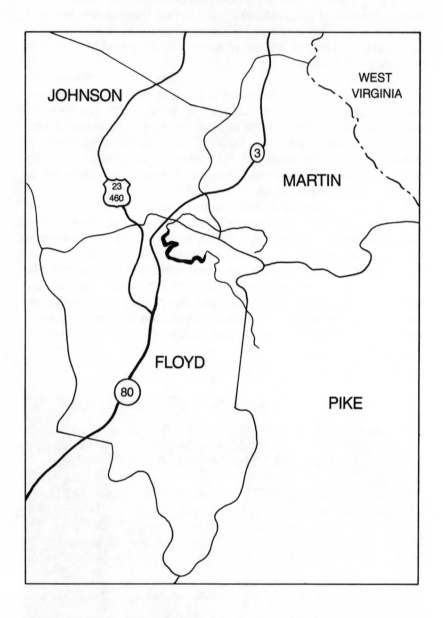

Dewey Lake

Location

Dewey Lake is approximately 120 miles east of Lexington in Floyd County, just a few minutes east of Prestonsburg. Opened to the public in May 1951, the lake was built under the authority of the Huntington, West Virginia, District of the U.S. Army Corps of Engineers. Construction of the project was initiated in March 1946.

The lake was impounded from John's Creek. The damsite is 3 miles upstream from its confluence with the Levisa Fork of the Big Sandy River. The main access highways to Dewey Lake are Interstate-64, US-23/460, Ky-3, Ky-1107, Ky-304 and Ky-194. The cost of the project was $7.8 million.

The 18.5-mile-long impoundment can be found on the U.S. Geological Survey topographic quadrangle (1/24,000 scale) for Lancer.

- No-Wake Embayments: Big Branch, Brandy Keg Creek, Dicks Creek and German Ridge
- Outboard Motor Size Restrictions: None

Size

Dewey Lake has 52 miles of shoreline at seasonal pool. The dam controls runoff from a drainage area of 207 square miles. At its deepest point, just above the dam, the lake is approximately 50 feet deep.

At summer pool, Dewey Lake reaches an elevation of 650 and has 1,100 surface acres; the winter drawdown reduces the lake to 16.8 miles in length and approximately 900 surface acres at elevation 645. Total storage capacity of the impoundment is 81,000 acre-feet.

For more information write: Resource Manager, Dewey Lake, U.S. Army Corps of Engineers, Route 1, Van Lear, KY 41265, or telephone (606) 437-7496.

Marinas

At this writing, there is only one marina on Dewey Lake—the Jenny Wiley State Resort Park Marina at Brandy Keg off Ky-304. On October 9,

1982, fire destroyed the Terry Boat Dock, which was located 6 miles north of Prestonsburg on Ky-1107, off US-23.

The Jenny Wiley State Resort Park Marina is open year-round and has approximately 75 boat slips, all open. There's a snack bar on the dock which is open seasonally, serving breakfast, sandwiches and coffee. Fishing boats can be rented, with or without the 9-horsepower outboards. Live bait, tackle and artificial lures are available, as are regular gas and a boat-launching ramp. For more information write: Jenny Wiley State Resort Park Marina, Prestonsburg, KY 41653, or telephone (606) 886-2711.

Fishing

Dewey Lake is a study in contradiction. While some say that the thirty-two-year-old impoundment has lost its ability to offer quality fishing, there are local anglers who routinely catch impressive strings of bass, and with the introduction of the tiger muskie, the mountain lake appears to be undergoing a change for the better.

Unfortunately, some sections of the lake suffer from silting caused by extensive surface mining in the Big Sandy River drainage. Silting isn't new to eastern Kentucky. Several impoundments in the coalfield, most notably Fishtrap Lake, are plagued with this problem. Consequently, heavy rains in late winter and spring cause Dewey Lake to muddy up; yet most of the time throughout the summer and fall it is clear, so clear that in the shallow flats at the upper end of the lake there's considerable weed growth.

Kerry Prather, Eastern District fishery biologist for the Kentucky Department of Fish and Wildlife Resources, explained that "the weed beds are in the upper third of the lake. *Ceratophyllum*, which is commonly called coontail, is growing where light penetrates to the bottom in the shallow flats adjacent to the river channel." Prather said that there are no plans to try to eradicate the weed beds. "They provide excellent cover for bass and muskellunge, and don't pose any navigational hazard. Some big fish are taken from those weed beds because they're close to the deep water of the old river channel."

Introduction of the tiger muskie, a sterile cross between a male northern pike (*Esox lucius*) and a female silver muskellunge (*Esox masquinongy ohioensis*), is breathing new life into the lake. More die-hard muskie anglers from across the state are fishing the impoundment each year as the numbers of harvestable fish increase. After six years of stocking the lake, beginning in 1975, the program is now in its evaluation stage.

"The largest fish stocked prior to this year [1982] were only 6 inches long," Prather said, adding that "the survival rate for intermediates is considerably better than for fry, or even fish up to 4 or 6 inches." No tiger muskie were stocked in Dewey Lake in 1976, although after 1977 the stocking rate was at least one fish per acre. In 1982 the stocking rate was approximately four fish per acre; 3,238 of the tiger muskies placed in the lake were between 8 and 11½ inches in length. The first stocking class in 1975 consisted of 515 6-inch fish.

Dewey Lake has already yielded a state record tiger muskie that weighed 13 pounds, 12 ounces and was 34 inches in length. The fish was caught on May 5, 1981, by James Mollet. There have been scattered, unconfirmed reports that tiger muskie in excess of 40 inches have been taken from Dewey Lake. These fish, which would have topped the record, were not officially verified. As for the future, it's likely that the fishery will expand now that larger fish have been stocked in recent years.

The forage base is adequate, Prather said, since the lake supports large numbers of golden redhorses (*Moxostoma erythrurum*) and northern hog suckers (*Hypentelium nigricans*), known locally as "hog mollies." Prather suggests that the best time of the year to fish for tiger muskies is in the spring between March 1 and the end of April. "If you can plan your trip to coincide with the sucker spawn in the headwaters of the lake, you'll have no trouble finding those tigers. They'll be right with the suckers in the shallow, riffle areas where creeks enter the lake."

Dalton Conley, the Floyd County conservation officer for the Kentucky Department of Fish and Wildlife Resources, who has worked the lake since its impoundment, said that the silt load has played havoc on the reproductive potential of the white bass in Dewey Lake. Prather concurred. "There appears to be low egg survival. A white bass study is planned for the future," he said, adding that "one thing we know for sure is that fishing pressure for white bass is very light."

Fish attractors, twenty-by-twenty-foot brush piles, have been placed in Dewey Lake during the past few years in the following embayments: mouth of McQuire Branch, Shade Branch, Stratton Branch, Burchett Branch, and two points on the main lake just above the dam. Fish attractor buoys, pinpointing the location of these brush piles, are slated to be placed in the lake during the spring of 1983. For a map of the fish attractor sites in Dewey Lake write: Kentucky Department of Fish and Wildlife Resources, 1 Game Farm Road, Frankfort, KY 40601, or telephone (502) 564-4336.

Crappie run small in Dewey Lake, although Prather thinks that predation by the tiger muskies is responsible for "the trend towards larger fish, ones in excess of the six-to-seven-inch average length we've had in past

Dewey Lake—photo by author

years." Deadfalls and brush piles in the upper end of the lake offer some of the best crappie fishing cover, since the impoundment doesn't have any flooded standing timber. One curiosity of the upper end of the lake is a small grove of cypress trees. Apparently they were planted by a local bass club. Imagine seeing cypress trees growing in a highland reservoir!

Dewey Lake also apparently has some sizable catfish, which prowl the shallow, mud-bottomed flats adjacent to the old river channel above German Bridge. It's a jug fisherman's paradise, and ideal for trotlines set parallel to the channel, utilizing plastic jugs for floats and anchors to keep the mainline just off the bottom. Channel catfish are the predominant species.

The bass fishery seems concentrated, for the most part, in several embayments of the lake. During samplings by electrofishing, Prather and his crew have rolled some good-sized bass in Copperas Creek, Clark's Branch, Dicks Creek and Big Branch. Prather cautions not to pass up the scattered weed beds in Big Branch. "We shocked up a couple of real beauties from those weeds this summer [1982]," he said.

Jig fishing with live nightcrawlers, flippin' jig and worm combinations and a Deep South technique called "jigger-bobbin" are all frequently used by local anglers on Dewey Lake when the water's discolored in the spring by rains. Jigger-bobbin' is similar to jig fishing in that it requires a long pole, a short length of heavy monofilament line and something to lure the fish into striking. In jigger-bobbin' a Lunker Lure or Mister Twister is used instead of live bait, but the technique is the same. Drag the lure back and forth amid likely looking bass cover and try to intimidate the bass into striking.

Prather said that by far the number-one lure for largemouth bass is the white spinnerbait, rigged with either white blades or silver blades. The spinnerbait is tops, with the "shad mimic baits," such as the Rebel Shad and Thin Fin Shad, and other crankbaits, like the A.C. Shiner, a close second. There aren't any smallmouth bass in Dewey Lake, but spotted bass abound. Trolling with crankbaits over deep rock points and fishing these areas slowly and carefully with four-inch electric grape augertail worms and ⅛-to-⅜-ounce jigs will put the "spots" in the live well.

Even though Dewey Lake offers limited bass, crappie and catfish angling opportunities, it's the emerging tiger muskie fishery that will bring the lake to prominence. This remarkable hybrid, which exhibits about the same growth rate as silver muskies until it reaches about thirty-six inches in length, first reached the thirty-inch minimum size limit in Dewey Lake in the summer of 1979.

The greenish stripes down the side, white belly and dark back make the fish distinctively attractive. As for growth potential and value as a sport fish consider that the IGFA all-tackle world record for the species is 51 pounds, 3 ounces. The monster tiger muskie was caught on July 16, 1919, by John A. Knobla from Lake Vieux-Desert on the Michigan-Wisconsin border.

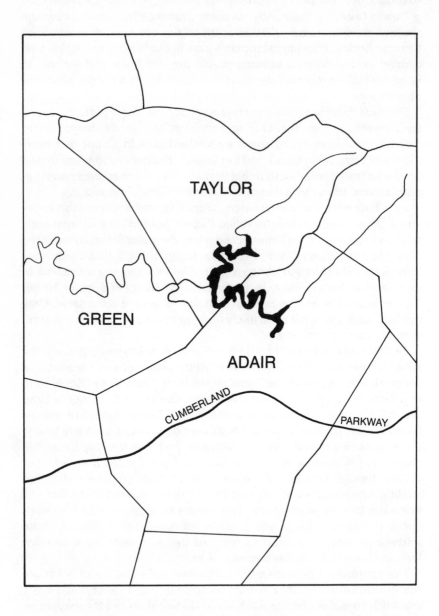

TAYLOR

GREEN

ADAIR

CUMBERLAND   PARKWAY

Green River Lake

Location

Green River Lake is approximately 77 miles southwest of Lexington in Taylor and Adair counties, reached via US-68, Ky-372, Ky-1061, Ky-682, Ky-551, Ky-206 and Ky-76. The damsite is approximately 26 miles upstream from Greensburg, 305.7 miles above the mouth of the Green River.

Completed in June 1969, the lake is east of Ky-55 between Campbellsville and Columbia. The cost of the project was $33.1 million. Green River Lake and surrounding recreational lands are found on the following U.S. Geological Survey topographic 1/24,000 scale quadrangles: Campbellsville, Cane Valley, Knifley, Columbia and Mannsville.

- No-Wake Embayments: None
- Outboard Motor Size Restriction: None

Size

At summer pool, elevation 675, the lake has 8,210 surface acres, is 25 miles long, and has 147 miles of shoreline. The winter drawdown reduces the lake to 6,650 surface acres at elevation 664. Green River Lake was built under the authority of the Louisville District of the U.S. Army Corps of Engineers.

For more information write: Resource Manager, Green River Lake, U.S. Army Corps of Engineers, Route 5, Campbellsville, KY 42718, or telephone (502) 465-4463.

Marinas

There are three marinas on Green River Lake—Holmes Bend Boat Dock, Taylor County Boat Dock and Green River Marina.

Holmes Bend Boat Dock is north of Columbia on Holmes Bend Road, off Ky-551. The marina is open April 1 to October 31. Rental boats include 40- and 50-foot houseboats, 28-foot pontoon boats with 35-horsepower outboards and 14-foot aluminum fishing boats with 6-to-9.5-horsepower outboard motors. Tackle, live bait, ice, snacks and fuel are available at the dock. For more information write: Holmes Bend Boat Dock, Route 1, Columbia, KY 42728, or telephone (502) 384-4425.

The Taylor County Boat Dock is 3 miles east of Campbellsville off Ky-372. Open twenty-four hours a day, March through November, the marina has a short-order counter. The rental 40-foot houseboat with a 50-horsepower outboard sleeps six. Fourteen-foot aluminum fishing boats with 6-to-7.5-horsepower outboards can also be rented, and the price includes life preservers and cushions. There are 20 covered, 5 open, 22 houseboat slips and numerous buoy tie-offs. Live bait (minnows, nightcrawlers and crickets), fishing tackle and fuel (mixed and regular gas) are also available. For more information write: Taylor County Boat Dock, Box 282, Campbellsville, KY 42718, or telephone (502) 465-3412.

Green River Marina is the state-owned but privately leased dock that adjoins Green River Lake State Park. It is open February through mid-December from 6:00 A.M. to midnight, and has 150 boat slips, 20 of which are covered. Live bait, crickets, red worms, minnows and nightcrawlers are available. The rental fleet features 14-foot aluminum fishing boats with 9.5-horsepower outboards, 24-foot pontoon boats with 40- and 50-horsepower outboards and houseboats, 40-, 50- and 53-footers powered by 85- and 100-horsepower outboards. Reservations require a deposit. The marina restaurant specializes in breakfast and short orders. For more information write: Green River Marina, Campbellsville, KY 42718, or telephone (502) 465-2512.

Fishing

One of the best-kept fishing secrets of Kentucky's major lakes is the fabulous smallmouth bass fishery at Green River Lake.

While Dale Hollow Lake, Lake Cumberland and Kentucky Lake are considered the state's top smallmouth lakes, many quality "brown bass" are taken each year from Green River Lake. Since the all-tackle world record smallmouth was caught from Dale Hollow Lake, it gets most of the attention in outdoor magazines, although I would venture a guess that there aren't many impoundments that could match up with Green River Lake in smallmouth production.

It seems logical to me that the admittedly poor forage base in the lake contributed to the success of the smallmouth by working against the growth of largemouths in the years immediately following impoundment. The boom in largemouth bass fishing that most new lakes experience never really materialized at Green River Lake. Southwest District fishery biologist Bonny Dale Laflin, who manages the impoundment, said that the lake drew lots of unfavorable publicity for the large numbers of small bass taken during the years immediately following impoundment.

Consequently, fishing pressure never has been as great as it is on other major lakes across the state, and attempts to bolster the forage base with threadfin shad have failed owing to the susceptibility to ice-overs of this relatively shallow lake. In any event, Laflin said that he thinks spotted bass may be more numerous in the lake than large-mouths, and that the smallmouth occupies better than 40 percent of the total bass fishery.

A top bass angler on the impoundment is Tom Williams of Campbells-ville, who has fished Green River Lake hard since it was built. He walked the lake bed prior to impoundment and has studied aerial photographs as well as old maps. A year-round angler, Williams says he has caught and released hundreds of smallmouth.

"My best day ever on the lake was Thanksgiving Day, 1978, when I caught and released thirteen fish. Two were smallmouths. One was 5 pounds, the other 5½ pounds. Eleven of the bass were largemouths be-tween 4 and 6½ pounds; the others averaged 3 pounds each," Williams recalls as a grin brightens his face.

Williams says that to the best of his knowledge the largest smallmouth ever taken from Green River Lake was a 9-pounder. The lunker was caught on a spinnerbait the third week in April from a gravel flats across from the dam. Williams is convinced that there's a new world record smallmouth, a fish approaching 12 pounds, in Green River Lake. The biggest largemouth ever taken from Green River Lake is thought to be a 10½-pounder caught the first week in September 1977 by an angler trolling a bomber along the old river channel near Holmes Bend.

It's not uncommon to harvest all three bass species during one outing, especially during the spring or fall peak fishing periods. January and February are slow fishing months, as expected, but by March fishing for largemouths is good to excellent by flippin' or jig fishing the southern exposed banks near deep water. Both split tail or chunk pork rinds on black doll flies are effective. Some largemouths are caught on spinner-baits fished very slowly. Fishing for smallmouth is good on the rocky points of the main lake using doll flies and pork rind combinations.

April is the best smallmouth month by far, Williams says, since the fish concentrate in spawning areas. "Three-to-six-pound fish are common," he said, pointing out that there are three top lures—jig and pork rind combinations, small spinnerbaits and crankbaits in crayfish patterns. Fish the rock points south of the dam thoroughly.

The Model-A Bomber is the number-one crankbait, followed by the deep and double-deep Rebel Wee-R. During this time big largemouths are caught by flippin' and casting crankbaits along brush and stump lines on points. During May smallmouth fishing continues to be excellent, with the crankbait a top lure choice. Rocky points, gravel bars and flats are the preferred cover. The smallmouth spawn is usually over by the second week of the month. There's also excellent fishing for largemouths at this time of the year in the backs of embayments over logs, stumps and brush. Many six-to-eight-pound fish are taken by anglers casting shallow-running crankbaits and Rapala-type balsa lures worked slowly.

Williams suggests fishing for smallmouth in June on overcast rainy days with spinnerbaits. "The postspawn largemouths are on the points, and some good catches are made on top-water lures such as the Cordell Boy Howdy and Lunker Lure," he explained. The hot weather of July and August is best spent fishing at night. Williams has had luck in the past fishing the drops with plastic worms, and the riprap along the dam face.

"I like to fish the clear nights when there's a quarter moon. The largemouths are in four to five feet of water, while the smallmouths are often on the very shallow gravel flats adjacent to the old river channel. A black or crayfish-colored spinnerbait is my top lure choice for night fishing," he said. The coming of autumn brings the top-water lures back into action, and largemouths are taken in the mornings and evenings. Occasionally, large smallmouths are taken by trolling in the main lake.

October is Williams's favorite month. "I have taken many limits of three-to-four-pound largemouths on crankbaits, and on overcast days some nice smallmouths off the rocky points," he said, adding that "I cast crankbaits and jig and pork rind combinations in November and December, after the drawdown." Flippin' is also a productive technique during this time of the year.

Williams's favorite crankbait in clear water at Green River Lake is the Tennessee Shad in the light crayfish pattern. The plastic worm he prefers is the 6-inch skinny striker in brown with an orange tail. Black and brown are top choices for jig and pork rind combinations, and Williams prefers to use ⅜-ounce jigs on 12-to-14-pound test line in the day, and 17-pound test at night.

His jigging rig consists of a 2/0 treble hook, chartreuse rubber skirt, float, nightcrawler and ½-ounce sinker. In March, Williams suggests fishing in about twelve feet of water. In April the first fish begin to move onto the stump rows along the old river channel.

Crappie, white bass, catfish and bluegill are also caught in great numbers from the lake, but in recent years the stockings of tiger muskie and silver muskie have made the major management news. The upper sections of Robinson Creek and Wilson Creek offer excellent white bass fishing in the spring, while my favorite summertime area of the lake for trolling is the submerged roadbed between the launching ramps at Pike Ridge and Smith Ridge. "Crappie are really coming on in the lake. During the last two years, the fishing has been excellent during the spring in and around flooded willows. Last year [1981] the crappie catch was estimated at 100,000 fish," Laflin said.

Beginning in 1977 there were massive stockings of muskie, 14,400 six-to-eight-inch fingerling silver muskies; in 1979–80 there were 17,213 six-inch tiger muskies released in the lake. The five-year program is now in its evaluation stage, following exhaustive age and growth studies.

Assistant Director Ted Crowell, however, characterizes the fishery as "limited or nonexistent." While a few adult muskies are taken from the lake each year, the fishery never panned out the way it was supposed to. The fingerlings that were stocked were evidently heavily preyed upon by bass. Since silver muskie are indigenous to the Green River basin, it's understandable that they would do better in the impoundment than the tiger muskies, but it's not known exactly why the tigers did so poorly.

At this writing the muskie program at Green River Lake is uncertain, as it hasn't been determined whether or not the investment of time, money, manpower and forage necessary to raise muskie up to thirteen to fifteen inches is cost effective. Biologists know that if a fishery is to be established, it's going to take massive stockings of fish that are large enough to escape predation.

"We raised approximately 2,000 silver muskie up to this intermediate size in a seven-acre brooder pond at the hatchery [Minor E. Clark], feeding them small goldfish. They were electrofished up and transported by truck to the lake in October of 1982," Crowell said, adding that "only time will tell whether or not we will continue the program."

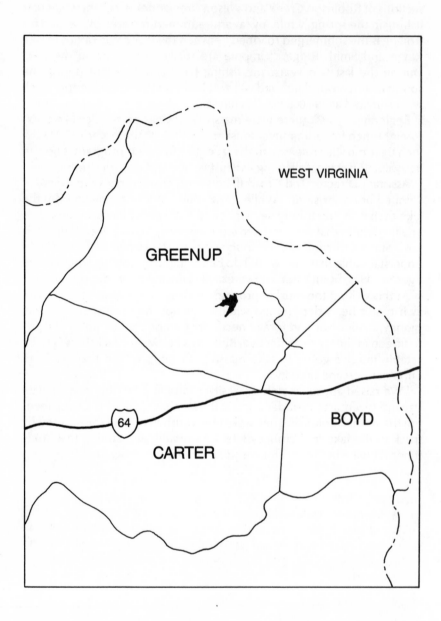

WEST VIRGINIA

GREENUP

BOYD

64

CARTER

Greenbo Lake

Location

Greenbo Lake is approximately 107 miles east of Lexington, just about a thirty-minute drive from Ashland in Greenup County. It can be reached via Interstate-64, US-23, Ky-1 and Ky-207.

The lake, and the surrounding 3,369 acres in Greenbo Lake State Resort Park can be found on the U.S. Geological Survey topographic quadrangle in 1/24,000 scale for Argillite and Oldtown.

- No-Wake Embayments: None
- Outboard Motor Size Restrictions: No motor larger than 7.5 horsepower

Size

Greenbo Lake is a 192-acre impoundment with little or no pool fluctuation. It is really just a big pond, as it isn't fed by any streams of substantial size, although runoff enters the lake at several points after heavy rains. The dam is earthen fill with a concrete spillway.

For more information write: Greenbo Lake State Resort Park, Greenup, KY 41144, or telephone (606) 473-7324, marina extension 543.

Marinas

The 70-slip state-owned-and-managed marina on Greenbo Lake is open April 1 to October 31, although unseasonably cold and rainy weather or lack of business can lead to an early closing. The fishing boats, 14-footers with 6-horsepower outboards, can be rented at both daily and hourly rates, as can the rental canoes and 18-foot pontoon boats. Both mixed and regular gas is available, as is live bait (red worms, crickets and minnows) and fishing tackle. The boat-launching ramp is open year-round.

Fishing

Lunker largemouth bass are the drawing card of this remote mountain lake.

Even though Greenbo Lake is a "small" lake in the truest sense of the word, and has practically nothing in common with the vast man-made impoundments profiled in this book, any review of the state's angling opportunities would be incomplete without a mention of a body of water that has yielded two state record largemouth bass.

The history of Greenbo Lake is a curious one indeed, worth telling time and again. It's an astounding, but nonetheless true, story about a lake that some people thought might not even hold water, much less produce huge bass. From the time that funds for the lake were collected by the Greenbo Lake Association in 1955 and the actual site was studied, the project was heaped with criticism.

The idea for the lake originated at a public meeting of local bass fishermen in Russell, Kentucky, on the night of February 25, 1952. It was simply a matter of wanting to build a lake because about the only bass fishing waters around were creeks and tiny ponds. Bear in mind that at that time large man-made impoundments were not so common as they are today.

And who can blame those eager bassmen for wanting some place close by to wet a line for a few hours in the evening after work. But biologists said that the land was infertile and the banks much too steep to provide adequate spawning sites. It was debatable whether the narrow valleys would even hold water.

The report on the lake was none too good, yet by 1956 the dreams of the bassmen were a reality. The 192-acre impoundment, nestled amid 3,369 acres of wooded hills, had filled with spring rains and was stocked with largemouth bass and bluegill, and a twelve-inch size limit on bass was established.

The project had cost the $110,000 raised by the Greenbo Lake Association, plus $125,000 chipped in by the Kentucky Department of Fish and Wildlife Resources, for the design of the lake and construction of the earthen and concrete dam. The stage was set for an amazing story.

The key figure in the unfolding drama was a man named Delbert Grizzle, of nearby Flatwoods, who would prove that Greenbo Lake was a bass haven indeed. When not working for the Chesapeake & Ohio Railroad, Grizzle headed for the lake. He was one of the first anglers in Kentucky to perfect night-fishing tactics for bass, but it was really a matter of circumstances, more than choice. Grizzle worked during the day, and he had no choice but to fish when he could, which was mostly at night.

On the night of September 21, 1965, he took a state record 11-pound, 10-ounce bass out of the lake, roughly nine years after its impoundment. Only a few months later, however, his record was broken when a fish

Greenbo Lake—photo by Soc Clay

close to 12 pounds was taken from another small lake. Grizzle responded by besting the new record, boating a 13-pound, 8-ounce largemouth the following summer, August 3, 1966. And that's not the end of this "fish story"; Grizzle claims to have hooked two fish in Greenbo Lake that he thinks would weigh in the neighborhood of 15 pounds!

Grizzle's formula for success is pretty simple, but other techniques are equally productive. His record fish were taken on unweighted, six-inch plastic worms (his preferred colors are wine, black, blue, light blue and blue purple), cast to the bank and slowly retrieved. His cardinal rule is "be absolutely quiet, and if you get hung up, break your line rather than going to the bank."

Suggested lures for bass fishing in Greenbo Lake are jigging spoons, pig and jig combinations and black and brown sonar-type lures in early spring; shad or crayfish-pattern crankbaits and plastic worms in black and purple hues in summer; floating minnow-type surface lures in shad colors and pig and jig combinations in autumn; and in winter, the lures used from January to March, in early spring.

Successful patterns include fishing the shallows adjacent to drop-offs, the long tapering rock points and the heads of coves. In summer, fish at night only. Cast parallel to the bank with red, silver or shad-colored crankbaits. Work the weed beds in twelve feet of water.

There are also limited numbers of crappie, bluegill and channel catfish in the lake, but their presence is greatly overshadowed by the bass fishery. Greenbo Lake is first and foremost a bass lake.

It should be noted that Greenbo Lake has a 7.5-horsepower outboard motor size restriction. If you have a boat with a larger outboard motor, it's not necessary to remove your motor to fish Greenbo Lake or any other small lake with such regulations. Simply trim up your outboard motor and use your trolling motor. While you're on the lake, it's illegal even to start a motor that's larger than the size restriction.

Photo courtesy of Mercury Marine

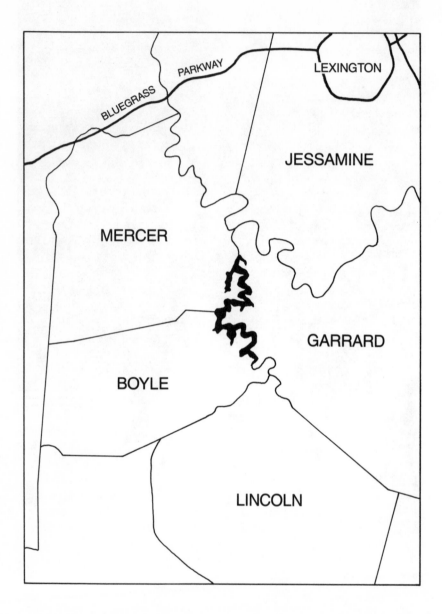

LEXINGTON

BLUEGRASS PARKWAY

JESSAMINE

MERCER

GARRARD

BOYLE

LINCOLN

Herrington Lake

Location

Herrington Lake is approximately 30 miles south of Lexington, forming the boundary between Mercer, Garrard and Boyle counties. Built in 1923 by the Kentucky Utilities Company primarily for the generation of hydroelectric power, Herrington Lake filled in the spring of 1925. It was the first large-scale impoundment built in Kentucky.

A 287-foot-high, 1,080-foot-long concrete dam impounds the Dix River approximately one mile upstream of its confluence with the Kentucky River at High Bridge. The lake is east of Harrodsburg, and accessible via Ky-33, Ky-152, Ky-34, US-127 and US-27.

Herrington Lake can be found on the following U.S. Geological Survey topographic quadrangles in 1/24,000 scale: Bryantsville and Wilmore.

- No-Wake Embayments: Cane Run and Tanyard Branch
- Outboard Motor Size Restriction: None

Size

Herrington Lake has about 92 miles of shoreline and 1,860 surface acres. The 35-mile-long impoundment reaches elevation 730 at summer pool; the winter drawdown reduces the lake to 1,200 surface acres at elevation 715. Total storage capacity of the impoundment is 3,600 surface acres, at elevation 760. The lake is 235 feet deep just above the dam.

For more information on Herrington Lake write: Supervisor's Office, Herrington Lake, E.W. Brown Generating Station, Box F, Burgin, KY 40310, or telephone (606) 748-5221. At this writing, no four-color recreation maps or reliable information on facilities is available for free distribution to the public.

Marinas

The following nine marinas on Herrington Lake are open to the public on a regular basis. There are numerous semi-private docks, not listed here, which are open somewhat seasonally or at the owner's whim. If a marina doesn't have a telephone, it won't be listed. Additionally, one

103

private condominium resort, Paradise Condominiums, telephone (606) 748-5504, has its own dock and sells gasoline to the public.

Bryant's Camp and Marina is 3 miles east of Danville on Ky-34 and is open April 1 to November 1. The marina has 30 open boat slips. Rental on the 14-foot fishing boats with 7.5-horsepower outboards includes one tank of gas, or the boats can be rented without motors. Regular and mixed gas, ice, launching ramp, tackle, live bait (red worms, minnows, crickets, nightcrawlers and meal worms), fish-cleaning station and freezer space are available. Breakfast, coffee and sandwiches are served at the restaurant from daylight to 9:00 P.M. daily. For more information write: Bryant's Camp and Marina, Box 397, Danville, KY 40422, or telephone (606) 236-5601.

King's Mill Marina is 6 miles south of Danville on Ky-34. Open year-round, the marina has 40 open slips and a snack bar on the dock (hot sandwiches, candy and soft drinks). The rental fishing boats, 14-footers, have 6.5-horsepower outboards. Regular gas, live bait (minnows, worms and crickets), ice, tackle, artificial bait and boat-launching ramp are available. For more information write: King's Mill Marina, Route 2, Lancaster KY 40444, or telephone (606) 548-2091.

Gwinn Island Fishing Camp is 3 miles northeast of Danville, off Ky-33. Open February 28 to November 30, the marina has 62 covered slips. There's a restaurant on the grounds (open Memorial Day to Labor Day, 6:30 A.M. to 9:00 P.M. daily). The rental on the fishing boats, 14-footers, includes three gallons of gas. The rental pontoon boats are 20-footers with 35-horsepower outboards. Fuel (regular and mixed), live bait (minnows, crickets and nightcrawlers), tackle, a fish-cleaning station and launching ramp are available. For more information write: Gwinn Island Fishing Camp, Route 2, Danville, KY 40422, or telephone (606) 236-4286.

Red Gate Camp, 11 miles north of Lancaster, Kentucky, is reached via US-27, Ky-753, and Tanyard Road. The marina is on Tanyard Branch, west of Bryantsville, Kentucky. Open twenty-four hours a day from March 1 to December 15, the marina has 25 open slips and a snack bar (hot sandwiches, soft drinks and candy). The 14-foot fiberglass fishing boats can be rented either with or without the 7.5-horsepower outboards. Rental lockers, regular gas, live bait (minnows, crickets, red worms and nightcrawlers), fish-cleaning station, freezer space, boat-launching ramp and covered 30-by-15-foot fishing dock are available. For more information write: Red Gate Camp, Route 4, Lancaster, KY 40444, or telephone (606) 548-3461.

Camp Kennedy Dock is 4 miles east of Burgin on Ky-152 at Kennedy Bridge. The marina is open year-round; the restaurant, which serves a full menu of foods, is open March 1 to November 30. The 49 covered

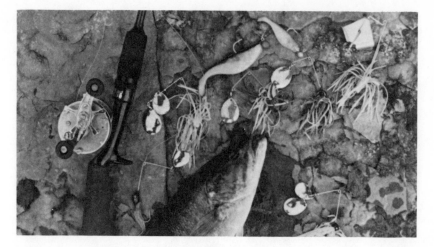

Smallmouth bass and lures—photo by author

slips are available for yearly rental only. The 50 open slips and buoy lines can be rented by the month or year. Rental boats include both 14-foot fishing boats with 6- or 9-horsepower outboards and 20-foot pontoon boats with 40-horsepower outboards. Regular and mixed gas, tackle, live bait (minnows, red worms and crickets), fish-cleaning station and boat-launching ramp are also available. For more information write: Camp Kennedy Dock, Box H, Burgin, KY 40310, or telephone (606) 548-2101.

Sunset Marina is 5 miles east of Burgin off Ky-152. Open year-round, the marina has 40 covered slips, a new tackle shop, candy, soft drinks, hot sandwiches and live bait—red worms, minnows and nightcrawlers. Rental on the 14-foot fishing boats with 5-horsepower outboards includes gas. For more information write: Sunset Marina, Route 4, Lancaster, KY 40444, or telephone (606) 548-3591.

Chimney Rock Resort, 8 miles east of Burgin on Ky-152, is open April 1 to November 1, weather permitting. The marina has 24 covered and 200 open slips, all rented by the week, month or year. Fishing boats, 14-footers, can be rented with 7-horsepower outboards. Ice, mixed and regular gas, live bait (worms, crickets and minnows), tackle and artificial baits, fish-cleaning station, candy and soft drinks and boat-launching ramp are available. For more information write: Chimney Rock Resort, Route 1, Harrodsburg, KY 40330, or telephone (606) 748-5252.

Freeman's Fishing Camp, open year-round, is 3 miles east of Burgin on Ky-152. The marina has 80 boat slips, 60 covered and 20 open. The rental 14- and 16-foot fiberglass fishing boats are equipped with 6-horsepower outboards. Sandwiches, soft drinks, snacks, handmade rods, tackle, regular and mixed gas, live bait (minnows, worms and crickets), fish-cleaning station and freezer space are available at the dock. The marina also offers outboard motor sales and service and boat and trailer sales. For more information write: Freeman's Fishing Camp, Route 1, Harrodsburg, KY 40330, or telephone (606) 748-5487.

Royalty's Fishing Camp is on the Curdsville Road off Ky-33 east of Burgin. Open year-round, there are 105 boat slips at the marina, 40 covered and 65 open. Soft drinks, candy, hot sandwiches, tackle and boating supplies are available at the dock. The fishing boats, 14-footers, have 6-horsepower outboards. Other facilities include mixed and regular gas, live bait (minnows, crickets and worms), boat-launching ramp, fish-cleaning station and freezer space. For more information write: Royalty's Fishing Camp, Route 4, Harrodsburg, KY 40330, or telephone (606) 748-5459.

Fishing

In the more than fifty-seven years since Herrington Lake was built, its popularity with fishermen has fluctuated about as much as its seasonal pool. The old lake has taken its share of criticism, yet fishery biologists will tell you that Herrington Lake is one of Kentucky's top five bass-producing lakes.

Fertile, limestone-rich waters and a tremendous forage base of brook silversides (*Labidesthes sicculus*) and gizzard and threadfin shad help support both the spotted bass and largemouth and an emerging small-mouth bass fishery. It's ironic that the lake's reputation was built on a white bass run that has now all but disappeared.

For a number of reasons, Herrington Lake is a difficult impoundment for bass fishermen to figure out. First of all, it's a deep lake with little shoreline cover other than rock ledges. Practically no timber was cut from the lake bed before the gates were closed on Dix Dam, but over the years most of it has rotted away, and wave action has exposed rock banks that are in most places practically straight up and down.

While spring's high water gets up into the tree line and floods drift-wood piles at the headwaters of most shallow embayments, for much of the year anglers have only deep rock structure to fish. And that's a tall order. Also, there's a theory that many largemouth suspend in the sub-merged treetops that are 15 to 25 feet down in the water column during summer pool.

Also contributing to the difficulty is increased water clarity and heavy pleasure-boat traffic. The most successful bass anglers have given up on fishing during the day in summer. If you want to catch a nice string of

White bass from Dix River (headwaters of Herrington Lake)—courtesy of Kentucky
Department of Fish and Wildlife Resources

Herrington Lake—courtesy of Kentucky Department of Fish and Wildlife Resources

bass during warm weather, you *must* fish at night, when motor oil, black, blue or purple plastic worms are the ticket to action.

On weekends it seems as though half of Lexington is on the lake, joy riding or water-skiing, and the lake simply isn't big enough to handle the people. To begin with, it's a long and narrow impoundment. Herrington Lake has remained a popular lake through convenience. Though privately owned by Kentucky Utilities Company (KU), the lake has always been open to the public in the fullest sense. No special permit is required for a dock or shanty boat on the lake; KU owns to elevation 760.

Since the establishment of the Kentucky Department of Fish and Wildlife Resources in the 1940s, the fisheries of Herrington Lake have been managed by state biologists. To correct out-of-balance fish populations, and better utilize the lake's forage, numerous game fish species have been introduced into the deep-water environment. Overall, it can be said that these stockings have had only mixed success.

Herrington Lake has always been known for its great white bass fishing. Up until the late 1950s it was just fantastic, but in the last two decades it has bottomed out. Why? Biologists aren't sure.

Traditionally, June signaled the beginning of casting the "jumps" and still-fishing minnows at night over gas lanterns. The plunker and fly, a great rig for catching white bass, is said to have been perfected here.

The white bass strikes the jig or fly, which is trailed on a leader behind a lipped stick bait. The rig is rapidly retrieved atop the water, simulating the action of a feeding bass. It is usually retrieved through a jump or blind cast in areas where fish have recently surfaced. At this writing, there are signs that the white bass fishery may be slowly recovering and that the lake is going through yet another cycle.

The species of game fish introduced into Herrington Lake include mostly predator fishes—walleye, northern pike and purebred rockfish— meant to utilize the massive schools of forage, and the cold deep-water environment. These introductions met with only limited success.

An overabundance of gizzard shad led to an eradication program in the early 1960s. Rotenone, supposedly administered at 1.0 part per million, killed millions of shad that were too big to be eaten by predator fish. Unfortunately, it also knocked out what was left of a declining smallmouth bass fishery.

In an attempt to reestablish smallmouth bass in Herrington, a three-year stocking program was initiated in 1979. That year, and in 1980, approximately 100,000 two-inch fingerlings were placed in the lake. In 1981 some of the fish stocked were intermediates, eight to nine inches in length. All of the fish came from a federal hatchery in Arkansas.

The evaluation stage of the project was begun at a time when bronze-backs started showing up more and more. Many of the smallmouth I caught in the autumn of 1982 were under twelve inches, but were fat and sassy. We can hope that the smallmouths will take hold in the lake.

Small plastic worms like the four-inch Lindy and six-inch grape Mann's augertail, ¼- and ⅛-ounce rubber-skirted jigs rigged with black pork frogs, ripple rind or split tails, and small crayfish-pattern crankbaits are topnotch lures. Be sure to fish the secondary points of the Rocky Fork embayment, near the dam, as they seem to be especially productive. The cold weather months are best for smallmouth. In late fall, as water temperatures approached 60 degrees Fahrenheit, I caught several small-mouth on small top-water propeller baits, twitched very slowly.

The walleye and northern pike stockings in the 1950s were incidental compared to the numbers of rainbow trout placed in Herrington be-tween 1967 and 1971. More than 50,000 six-inch trout were stocked in an attempt to establish a "two-story fishery." Biologists discontinued the program because the results didn't justify the effort.

The rockfish stocking program was perhaps the only fishery manage-ment project that ever brought Herrington Lake extensive coverage in the outdoor press. Throughout the 1960s, both rockfish fingerlings and fry were introduced into the lake. A predator for the large gizzard shad, the adult fish were expected to remedy a problem as much as to create a new sport fishery. The project was the pride and joy of Charlie Bowers, the now-retired director of fisheries for the Kentucky Department of Fish and Wildlife Resources.

About the same time that "stripers" were first introduced in Herring-ton, they were also experimentally stocked in Barren River Lake, Lake Cumberland and Kentucky Lake. The rockfish in Herrington Lake grew quickly to the 30-pound class. At one time the state record, a 44-pound, 4-ounce rockfish caught jointly by James Fugate and Ronald Warner on July 19, 1970, was claimed by Herrington.

But the fishery just didn't develop the way it was supposed to. Several quirks of the rockfish meant disaster for many of the trophy-sized fish. First, rockfish seek out water of 68 degrees Fahrenheit, and apparently will stay there regardless of the circumstances. Biologists determined that many of the fish were suffocating because at certain times of the year, 68-degree water in Herrington didn't have sufficient levels of dis-solved oxygen to support them.

Some fish, it is believed, literally starved to death, since they would stay in the optimal temperature band even if no shad were present. Also, for some unknown reason, the rockfish in Herrington often tried to swim through the hydroelectric turbines into the river. After conceding that the environment was marginal at best for the rockfish, the department discontinued the stocking program.

The rockfish–white bass hybrid has been introduced into Herrington and is apparently adapting well because it thrives in habitat that is marginal for the pure-bred rockfish and acceptable to the white bass. Rockfish–white bass hybrids weighing in excess of four pounds have been caught from Herrington Lake.

Anglers equipped with graph recorders to help in the location of forage schools and suspended fish have a tremendous advantage. Trolling is a top technique, as well as casting the jumps in early summer. White bombers with trailer spoons on eighteen inches of leader make a good trolling rig, as does shad-pattern crankbaits, especially the Rebel Shad series. Stick baits and spoons, like the Mepps jeweled-finish series, are excellent choices for casting the jumps.

In 1965 threadfin and shad were introduced into Herrington from Lake Cumberland. Since these shad only grow to about two inches in length, they can easily be taken by white bass and all three species of black basses in the lake. Susceptible to cold weather, the threadfin have drastically declined in all of Kentucky's lakes except Herrington because of recent harsh winters. Thus, the lake has become the supplier of fish for stocking in other lakes. The threadfin are taken in nighttime netting operations conducted by biologists.

Bluegill also are highly sought after. They are caught in great numbers off rocky points and in flooded treetops. Crickets are the top bait, but wax worms, meal worms, bag worms, horseweed worms and catalpa worms are also used effectively. When summer's swelter hits, the big bluegills go deep, and that's the time to drift fish along the steep rock walls of the main lake from Geary's Hollow to the mouth of Rocky Fork at the dam. Be sure to fish the main points.

One of the best ways to locate structure (ledges, submerged treetops and gradually sloping points) is to tour the lake in the winter when the water's down. Since Herrington Lake fluctuates so drastically, likely looking crappie and bluegill "holes" can be easily discovered, as well as prime spots to worm fish for bass. The "hogback" at Dunn Island, McKechnie Branch and Dennie's Branch of Cane Run Creek are three personal favorite sections of the lake for bass fishing.

When the water's down, it's easy to find banks that are devoid of cover. On Herrington Lake that's a big advantage—eliminating the nonproductive areas first, before you even pick up your rod and reel. It will save you lots of time and help you better appreciate a highly misunderstood lake that continues to produce some excellent fishing for the angler who sticks it out.

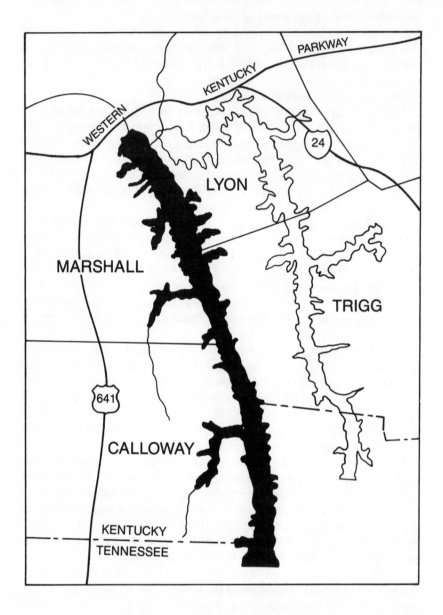

WESTERN

KENTUCKY PARKWAY

24

LYON

MARSHALL

TRIGG

641

CALLOWAY

KENTUCKY
TENNESSEE

Kentucky Lake

Location

Kentucky Lake is approximately 15 miles southeast of Paducah in Marshall, Lyon, Calloway and Trigg counties. The dam, a 20-story, 8,422 foot-long structure that impounds the nation's fifth largest river, was six years in construction. Between July 1, 1938, and August 30, 1944, as many as five thousand men worked on the project. The damsite is 25 miles upstream from the Tennessee River's confluence with the Ohio River.

The west bank of the lake is accessible via Interstate-24, US-641, Purchase Parkway, Ky-1422, Ky-963, Ky-58, Ky-962, US-68, Ky-80, Ky-732, Ky-280, Ky-444 and Ky-121. The cost of the project was $118 million.

The lake can be found on the following TVA navigational maps: 101, 102, 103 and 104 in the scale of 1 foot equals ½ mile; or the following U.S. Geological Survey topographic quadrangles in 1/24,000 scale: Birmingham Point, Briensburg, Buchanan, Calvert City, Fairdealing, Fenton, Grand Rivers, Hamlin, Hico, Mont, Paris Landing, New Concord and Rushing Creek.

- No-Wake Embayments: None
- Outboard Motor Size Restrictions: None

Size

Kentucky Lake was built by the Tennessee Valley Authority, and was the first of the two "sister" lakes (the other is Lake Barkley) that surround Land Between the Lakes (LBL), the 170,000-acre national recreation and demonstration area authorized by the late President John F. Kennedy. A 184-mile-long impoundment with 2,400 miles of shoreline (at summer pool), Kentucky Lake roughly parallels Lake Barkley for more than 40 miles.

There are 160,300 surface acres, 49,511 of which are in Kentucky. At summer pool, Kentucky Lake reaches an elevation of 359 feet above sea level; the winter drawdown reduces the lake to 128,900 surface acres at elevation 354.

For more information write: Kentucky Lake, TVA, Natural Resource Operations, Box 280, Paris, TN 38242, or telephone (901) 642-2041.

Marinas

There are 11 marinas on Kentucky Lake, north of the Tennessee-Kentucky boundary.

The largest state-owned marina complex in the Kentucky State Park System is at Kentucky Dam, adjacent to the lodge. There is a total of 277 boat slips, 177 of which are covered. The marina is open year-round. Rental fishing boats, 14-footers with 8-horsepower outboards, and 24-foot pontoon boats with 40-horsepower outboards are available.

The 42-foot houseboats are powered by 120-horsepower inboards. Off-season and split-week "specials" are available. The houseboats are fully equipped—three-burner ranges, icebox, sink, lavatory, linens, blankets, dishes, life jackets, cooking utensils, pots and pans, glassware and wall-to-wall carpeting. All visitors need to bring is fishing gear, personal items and clothing, and food.

A full line of boating and fishing supplies, tackle, live bait (minnows, worms, crickets and cut bait) and snacks are available at the marina. A launching ramp, fish-cleaning area and overnight freezer space are provided for guests. For more information write: Kentucky Dam Marina, Route 1, Gilbertsville, KY 42044, or telephone (502) 362-8500.

The Moors Resort and Marina, open year-round on a limited basis, is 8½ miles south of Kentucky Dam on Ky-963 off US-68. The marina has 116 slips, 90 covered and 26 open. The rental fleet includes 16-foot fishing boats with 6-horsepower outboards and 26-foot pontoon boats with 40-horsepower outboards. Regular and mixed gas and live bait (minnows, worms and crickets) are available. There's also a boat-launching ramp, fish-cleaning station, limited freezer space, dry-dock service and outboard motor mechanic on duty. For more information write: Moors Resort and Marina, Route 2, Gilbertsville, KY 42044, or telephone (502) 362-4356.

The Big Bear Resort Marina is located where Ky-58 dead-ends at the Bear Creek embayment, 8 miles northeast of Fairdealing, off US-68. Open April 1 to November 1, the marina has 100 boat slips, 28 of which are covered. Sixteen-foot bass boats with 35-horsepower outboards, 14-foot aluminum fishing boats equipped with 6-to-15-horsepower outboards and 22-foot pontoon boats can be rented. Gas, tackle, outboard motor service, live bait (minnows, crickets and red worms), a fish-cleaning station and freezer space (for use by guests) are available. A launching ramp adjoins the marina. For more information write: Big Bear Resort, Route 4, Box 156, Benton, KY 42025, or telephone (502) 354-6414.

The Hester's Spot in the Sun Marina is 3 miles east of Fairdealing, Kentucky, off Ky-962. Open from late March to mid-November, the marina is open at request twenty-four hours a day seasonally. The 14-foot

Kentucky Lake and Dam—courtesy of Kentucky Office of Tourism Development

aluminum fishing boats can be rented with either 6-horsepower out-boards or 15-horsepower outboards. The 25-foot pontoon boats have 50-horsepower outboards. Mixed and regular gas, live bait (minnows, crickets and red worms), a fish-cleaning station, freezer space and launching ramp are available for use by guests. For more information write: Hester's Spot in the Sun, Route 4, Benton, KY 42025, or telephone (502) 354-8280.

The Will-Vera Village Marina is reached via US-68 and Ky-962, 3 miles east of Fairdealing, Kentucky. Open March 1 to November 1, the marina has 90 boat slips, 30 of which are covered. Rental boats include both 14-foot fishing boats equipped with 9.9-horsepower outboards and 18-foot pontoon boats equipped with 40-horsepower outboards. Gas (both regular and mixed), live bait (minnows, crickets and red worms), a fish-cleaning station and freezer space are available. A launching ramp is next to the marina. For more information write: Will-Vera Village Marina, Route 4, Box 228, Benton, KY 42025, or telephone (502) 354-6422.

There are four marinas in the Jonathan Creek embayment, all within a three-mile radius of the US-68 bridge.

The Lakeside Camping Resort Marina is open twenty-four hours a day March 1 through October 31 and has 10 covered and 10 open slips. Both 14- and 16-foot aluminum fishing boats, equipped with 9.5-horsepower outboards and 24-foot pontoon boats are available. The marina has live bait (crickets, minnows, worms and cut bait), as well as a fish-cleaning station and freezer space. The boat-launching ramp is at the dock. For more information write: Lakeside Camping Resort Marina, Route 5, Benton, KY 42025, or telephone (502) 354-8157.

The Sportsman's Marina is open March 15 to November 1 and has 245 slips, 185 of which are covered. The rental fleet includes aluminum fish-ing boats, 14-footers with 9.5-horsepower outboards, 24- and 28-foot pontoon boats with 50- and 60-horsepower outboards, and 36- and 42-foot diesel-powered houseboats. A launching ramp is adjacent to the marina, which also supplies live bait (minnows, crickets, red worms and cut bait), mixed and regular gas, tackle, a fish-cleaning station, freezer space, and a boat wash. For more information write: Sportsman's Marina, Route 5, Box 418 A, Benton, KY 42025, or telephone (502) 354-6568.

The Town and Country Resort Marina has 80 boat slips, 50 of which are covered. Both fishing boats, 14- and 16-footers equipped with 9.5- and 15-horsepower outboards, and 24-foot pontoon boats with 40-horsepower outboards are available. Open year-round, the marina is also equipped for mixed and regular gas sales, fish cleaning (freezer space available to guests), live bait sales (minnows, crickets, red worms and cut bait) and has an adjoining launching ramp. Each boat slip is equipped for water and electric hookups and has its own individual locker. A floating patio is anchored at the dock for parties and cookouts. For more information write: Town and Country Resort Marina, Route 5, Benton, KY 42025, or telephone (502) 354-6587.

The Kenlake State Resort Park Marina, on Ledbetter Creek, has 210 slips, 160 covered and 50 open. Open year-round, twenty-four hours a day, the marina has a snack bar, a wide assortment of outdoor clothing, tackle, boating and fishing supplies, live bait (minnows, crickets, worms and cut bait), launching ramp, fish-cleaning area and freezer space, and mechanic on duty twenty-four hours. The 14-foot fishing boats are equipped with 9.5-horsepower outboards, while the 24-foot pontoon boats are powered by 35-horsepower outboards. For more information write: Kenlake State Resort Park Marina, Route 1, Hardin, KY 42048, or telephone (502) 474-2211, ext. 171.

The Blood River Dock, open April 1 to November 15, is 9 miles north of Murray and is reached via Ky-94 and Ky-280. The marina has 40 open slips and rents 14-foot fishing boats. Gas, fishing supplies and live bait (minnows, crickets and cut bait) are available. For more information write: Blood River Dock, Route 5, Murray, KY 42071, or telephone (502) 436-5321.

The Missing Hill Marina, open, weather permitting, April 1 to October 31, is about 15 miles southeast of Murray, off Ky-121, on the Cypress Creek embayment near the Tennessee-Kentucky border. The marina has 45 boat slips, 30 covered and 15 open. Rentals include 14-foot fishing boats with 9.5-horsepower outboards and 25-foot pontoon boats with 40-horsepower outboards. Mixed and regular gas, live bait (minnows, crickets and red worms), fish-cleaning station, freezer space and launching ramp are available. For more information write: Missing Hill Marina, Route 1, CR Box 215 A, New Concord, KY 42076, or telephone (502) 436-5519.

Fishing

Kentucky Lake, the state's second oldest impoundment, has a strong regional reputation for producing large numbers of quality game fish. Even though the crappie is by far the lake's number-one fish, stringers and stringers of largemouth, spotted and smallmouth bass, as well as catfish and sauger, are taken from the lake every year.

The crappie is one of the state's top game fish, and Kentucky Lake is *the* lake for the big, braggin'-size fish. White and black crappie are the bread-and-butter fish of many western Kentucky anglers, who live at the back door of one of three lakes in the United States that consistently produce big crappies. The others are Santee-Cooper in South Carolina and Toledo Bend on the Louisiana-Texas border.

Locally, crappie are called "slabs," although they are known as "new-lights," "specs," or "calico bass" in other parts of the country. By whatever name, when rolled in cornmeal, fried in hot oil and served with potato salad, baked beans, hush puppies and coleslaw, there's no finer eating. During the cold weather months, the crappie's flesh is especially sweet and firm.

Crappie fishing on Kentucky Lake is a way of life for many anglers—a serious pursuit for some, but just plain fun for the whole family. It isn't very complicated to master, the tackle is relatively simple compared to other kinds of fishing, and the catch is plentiful.

Both species of crappie are found in the lake. The white (*Pomoxis annularis*) and black (*Pomoxis nigromaculatus*) crappie vary only slightly in coloration most of the year. During spawning, however, black crappie often become extremely dark. Generally, white crappie grow to a larger size than black crappie, and are found in larger numbers.

Kentucky's state record crappie (there's no mention of whether the fish was a black or white crappie; evidently there's no distinction between the two species in the record books) was caught April 16, 1969, by David C. Crowe. The fish weighed 4 pounds, 3 ounces, and was taken from Lake Pewee in Hopkins County, in west central Kentucky.

The impact of the crappie fishery in Kentucky Lake is staggering indeed. For example, at a crappie fishing seminar in Gilbertsville in October 1980, Western District biologist Bill McLemore, of Kentucky's Department of Fish and Wildlife Resources, revealed some incredible findings from a creel survey conducted from mid-April 1978 to mid-March 1980.

McLemore said that it was estimated that anglers made 213,000 fishing trips and spent 917,000 hours on Kentucky Lake. About 411,000 fish were harvested, with a total weight of 328,000 pounds. Of the fish taken, the white crappie led all species in the creel. About 250,000 crappie were caught, for a total weight of 148,000 pounds. The crappie taken represented 61 percent of all fish caught, and 50 to 80 percent of all crappie taken were boated in the months of April and May.

In the early 1950s, a study on Kentucky Lake revealed that in five years the average crappie grew to about 13 inches with a weight of 1.5 pounds, with some weight and length variations. Literally hundreds of 3-pound crappie are harvested from Kentucky Lake each year. Two-pounders are common. Biologists know that the main reasons why crappie grow to such a large size here and in Lake Barkley are a quality forage fish supply and angler pressure. "Crappie tend to overpopulate and become

Crappie from Kentucky Lake—courtesy of Kentucky Office of Tourism Development

stunted if a large percentage of the population isn't removed each year," McLemore explained.

In March, before the crappie run begins, the best way to catch a handsome stringer of big slab crappie is by bouncing live minnows across stump rows and brush along deep-water drop-offs. Oftentimes the channels will hold the crappie, while the adjacent flats will hold sauger and spots. Deep-water crappie fishing isn't easy, but the hard work can pay off nicely. If a school of fish is located, it's possible to boat a washtub full of slabs in a matter of hours.

As in most deep-water angling, specialized gear must be used, and the angler must have knowledge of fish-holding structure. Knowing how to fish isn't what's hard to learn; it's where to find fish consistently. While Kentucky Lake enjoys a national reputation as a lake that produces big crappie, offering tremendous opportunities for the hard-working angler, there are nonetheless some unproductive waters. Knowing where to fish is half the battle.

Some top embayments on the west bank of Kentucky Lake for pre-spawn deep-water fishing are Taylor Creek, Bear Creek, Jonathan Creek, Ledbetter Creek, Blood River and Cypress Creek. Pisgah Bay, Vickers Bay and Barnett Creek on the east bank bordering Land Between the Lakes are also top crappie producers.

Bass fishing on Kentucky Lake—courtesy of Kentucky Office of Tourism Development

To be successful almost every trip out means spending a lot of time seeking out productive spots that you'll have all to yourself—humpbacks along the old river channel, rock piles, old fence rows, building foundations, or drop-offs cluttered with stumps and brush.

A little bit of cooperation from the weather helps. High winds, drops in the lake level and cold snaps play havoc on normal spring crappie patterns. Also, if the lake is whitecapping, it's difficult to position the boat and keep it steady so that the subtle bites of these fish can be felt. When the water's still cold, crappie don't really grab the bait; they move off with it in their mouths.

"About 95 percent of the time crappie will hold tight to the cover in 12 to 20 feet of water," said Harlyn Nall, a fishing guide working out of Sportsman's Marina on Jonathan Creek of Kentucky Lake. "They don't leave the deep water except to head for the flooded brush along the banks during the spawn."

"Sometimes you'll see them as a flash on the depth finder, suspended in the water column, but not very often," said Nall. "If you don't have a depth finder and think the crappie may be suspended, the best way to find them is to give your reel handle a couple of cranks so that the minnow is just off the bottom, fish awhile, then crank up some more, keeping track of the number of turns you are off the bottom. Once you've located the depth at which the fish are suspended," he went on, "it's simply a matter of letting your rig sink to the bottom, then reeling up the exact number of turns."

With a hydrographic map of the lake, a depth finder or graph recorder and some time to check out stretches of water that look good on paper, anyone can find crappie on Kentucky Lake, almost any time of the year. The wintry days of late fall are especially productive; some of the best fishing I've ever had on Kentucky Lake has come during this time of the year, when the locals have their minds on deer hunting and dry dock their boats until spring.

Of the literally hundreds of miles of submerged creek channels and stump rows in the lake, there are bound to be some choice spots that go unnoticed year after year.

There are two schools of thought concerning the proper tackle for deep-water crappie fishing. Some anglers believe that heavy line, 20-pound test monofilament, should be used so that the light wire 2/0 hooks can be pulled loose when the rig gets hung up on stumps and brush. The tandem rig has two drop lines (thus two hooks) and is weighted with an egg sinker. Usually, half-ounce weights are used in calm water, and the ounce size in wind or when fishing extremely deep.

The "Kentucky Lake crappie rigs" available in bait shops and marinas throughout western Kentucky were first handmade by "Dutch" Owens in the 1940s. Owens perfected the tackle and techniques for deep-water crappie fishing still used by fishermen today.

Known throughout the Southeast as the "father of deep-water crappie fishing," Dutch invented the "feel pole," a telescoping fiberglass rod with guides similar to a jigging pole, but with a piano wire tip. There's a small reel to hold the heavy monofilament line recommended for use with this super-sensitive crappie pole.

If you prefer not to buy ready-made rigs, you can make your own that will work just as well. All it takes is two three-way swivels, a bell-shaped (⅝ to 1 ounce) sinker, hooks and heavy monofilament leader. Tie the sinker on the bottom of the rig, with the swivels atop one another, connected by leader. Suspend the hooks from the drops.

Ultralight spinning gear is also used extensively in deep-water crappie fishing. Some fishermen say that the subtle hits of a crappie during the early spring can't be felt as easy with heavy gear. Four-, six- and

Kentucky Lake—photo by Soc Clay

eight-pound test line is used most frequently. The obvious drawback is that when you get hung up with light line, you'll probably lose the whole rig because the line will snap before the hook bends loose. Fortunately, these rigs are inexpensive to make. I personally prefer to use "gold" hooks, rather than those with a black finish.

Likewise, jigs will give you better action when they're fished on ultralight gear. When fishing in deep water, be sure to work jigs slowly, much as you would a plastic worm when bass fishing. Sometimes if you work the jig vertically, rather than cast out and reel in or backtroll, you'll catch more fish. Some anglers hook a live shiner minnow on their jigs, especially during the colder months, when the fish are sluggish. Pink and white, white or yellow seem to be the colors most preferred by crappie in the twin lakes during the spring.

Jigs that have been proven effective on crappie are the 1/16- and 1/8-ounce "roadrunner," "pinky" maribou jig, "slider heads," "fuzzy grub" and "sassy shad." Mepps spinners and doll flies are also good artificials for crappie. Remember, whether you're fishing with bait or artificials, the mouths of big crappie are paper thin, so be sure to have a landing net in the boat. Larger fish may tear loose if you try to horse them in.

There's a saying among oldtimers in western Kentucky and Tennessee that the "crappie will be on the banks when the oak leaves are the size of squirrel ears." Behind this folksy colloquialism is a lot of truth, since fishery biologists tell us that the combination of factors—air temperature, photoperiod and rainfall—that dictates the time when trees begin to bud out also signals, almost without fail, the time when crappie migrate into the shallows to spawn.

The two-to-three week spring crappie run at Kentucky Lake is a "main event" each year on many anglers' calendars. To borrow a saying from the racetrack, it's a time when everybody "gets well."

The big slabs, those crappie in the 1½-to-2½-pound class, have finished their migration from the deep creek channel drop-offs and swarm in the flooded willows, buck bushes and drift along the shoreline. There's a smile on every angler's face and a basket full of fish in every camp. The tackle is simple and the action is fast.

Crappie, like bluegill, are colony nesters. Where you find one spawning pair, you'll find many others. Unlike largemouth bass, the male crappie doesn't guard the nest for very long after the eggs hatch.

To catch a mess of fish during the spawning run all that's needed is a long cane pole or flyrod, rigged with 20-pound test monofilament leader, float, pea-sized split shot, 2/0 thin wire hook and lively minnow.

The heavy line and light hook allow the angler to pull hooks loose easier without losing them. When fishing heavy brush, you're bound to get hung up a lot. Just ease the boat along the flooded bushes using a scull paddle or electric trolling motor and drop the minnow in holes between the brush. If it sits for a few seconds and you don't get a strike, heft the pole up and drop your bait in another likely looking spot.

The long pole allows the angler to get the bait in hard to reach spots, as well as horsing out slab crappies so they don't have an opportunity to get your line tangled up in the brush. During this time, when the spawn's in full bloom, it's not uncommon for the crappie to be in water less than a foot deep, way back up in the bushes and drift piles. One crappie expert told me he's seen crappie spawning in water so shallow their dorsal fins showed.

During the spawning run most veteran crappie anglers prefer to fish with larger minnows than they use in early spring. When they're ready to go on the nest, crappie are aggressive, active feeders. The larger minnows also stay on the hook better and withstand the constant dunking.

During the spawn, crappie will take the bait the second it's put in front of their noses. Black crappie, which are not as plentiful as white crappie, take on a deep, almost solid black coloration during spawn. More large adult black crappie seem to be caught during the spawn than at any other time of the year.

Timing is the all-important ingredient in getting in on super crappie fishing. The Kentucky Lake Vacationland Association and the Marshall County Chamber of Commerce have established a "Fisherman's Hotline" to assist anglers by providing day-to-day reports of water temperature, area lake and river levels and extended weather forecasts. The service is available live from 9:00 A.M. to 5:00 P.M., Monday through Friday. At night and on weekends, there's a taped message. The "Fisherman's Hotline" number is (502) 527-7665.

The big slabs move into the shallows for just a couple of weeks, although they may linger in submerged creek channels (four to eight feet of water) of small embayments for a month or so. A cold snap may drive them out of the bushes, but they won't go far, at least not back into their deep-water haunts. They'll head for submerged creek channels in relatively shallow water, which can be fished easily with ultralights and jigs, as well as a cane pole, single hook and bobber rig with live minnows as bait.

While Kentucky Lake has always been considered to offer the best crappie fishing of western Kentucky's major impoundments, Lake Barkley was chosen as the site for a fish attractor program study. The problem with this type of impoundment, as biologists knew from creel data and personal communication with anglers, was that as the existing

Smallmouth and largemouth bass caught by Charley Taylor on Kentucky Lake—photo by Soc Clay

cover—brush, stump beds and timber—deteriorated, it became harder for the average angler to locate schools of fish.

The fish attractor study in September 1978 was a cooperative effort by fourteen fish and wildlife departments from the Southeast, several universities and federal agencies. The results were impressive, clearly proving that the placement of man-made fish shelters benefits crappie most of all, and other game fish to a lesser degree. For example, in the 207-acre study area on Crooked Creek embayment of Lake Barkley, one site—a one-acre brush attractor—yielded 575.8 pounds per acre, while a typical cove held only 4 pounds per acre and an open-water area 30.7 pounds per acre. With this simple and relatively inexpensive technique, quality crappie fishing could be assured for the future.

The study results prompted a major effort by the Kentucky Department of Fish and Wildlife Resources and fishery biologists of the Tennessee Valley Authority (TVA), to establish as many fish attractor sites on both lakes as possible with available manpower and materials. As one fishery administrator put it, "The goals of the program are to establish more clearly defined structure that both the fish and fisherman will recognize and use. We hope that they will concentrate fish and give anglers definite areas to concentrate their activity leading to a corresponding jump in angler success and total harvest."

The summer of 1982 marked the end of a five-year effort by Kentucky Department of Fish and Wildlife biologist Bill McLemore and his crew. Likewise, TVA fishery biologists have been placing both shallow- and deep-water attractors in embayments bordering Land Between the Lakes. The logo on each buoy at a fish attractor site is the outline of a fish approaching a hook.

TVA publishes a handy, pocket-sized map to the fish attractors they placed in Kentucky Lake and managed ponds in their 170,000-acre national recreation area. For more information write: Fish Attractor and Pond Map, TVA, Land Between the Lakes, Golden Pond, KY 42231, or telephone (502) 924-5602.

The sauger is another top fish in the eyes of those anglers who are in the sport for the meat instead of the glory. Sauger are delicious baked or fried, resembling walleye in taste and texture. And without question, the sauger is an underutilized game fish, even in Kentucky Lake, where they are fished for more than anywhere else in the state on our major impoundments.

They are a school fish, and that's good news for the angler intent on taking the limit of ten fish. Since sauger are cold-water fishes, the best fishing times are in the autumn, winter and early spring. Trolling crankbaits or bouncing jigs across shallow ridges and flats along the old river channel yields many sauger. Fish in eight to twelve feet of water, and be sure to keep your bait or lure right on the bottom, since sauger are lazy and won't venture far when chasing food. Fluorescent orange or yellow jigs and white or crayfish-pattern crankbaits are top choices.

Some of the best sections of Kentucky Lake for sauger are the sub-merged island flats from mile 25 of the Tennessee River at the Lake Barkley–Kentucky Lake Canal to mile 30, the mouth of Bear Creek, the mouth of Jonathan Creek, the mouth of Sugar Bay, the creek channel flats adjacent to Kenlake State Resort Park Marina in Ledbetter Creek, and the submerged island flats at the mouth of the Blood River embay-ment at mile 52 of the Tennessee River.

My favorite section of Kentucky Lake for largemouth bass fishing is the lower sixteen miles along the west bank—mainly Sledd Creek, Little Bear Creek, Bear Creek, Malcolm Creek and the mouth of Jonathan Creek. The stump beds, stake beds, brush pile fish attractors and gravel points are a bass paradise.

The resort operators in Bear Creek have sunk hundreds of brush piles and hammered in hickory and oak stake beds in the embayment, and the added cover has made the fishing excellent. The best time to fish Kentucky Lake, as far as I'm concerned, is when the newly spawned shad minnows are "in the bushes," during June. Throw a buzzbait in the morning, then shift to a crankbait or plastic worm later in the day.

Work the secondary points and shallow main lake points, especially the ones with stump beds, deadfalls or submerged willows adjacent to the old river channel. Be sure to fish the island at the mouth of Bear Creek. There's an old roadbed on the south side of the island that usually holds bass.

Also, don't pass up the numerous private boat houses on this section of the lake; they sometimes offer bonanzas of big fish in the spring. The big island just north of the mouth of Jonathan Creek is another hotspot. Fish the stump rows on the channel breakline with a buzzbait early, then switch to a plastic worm.

A new approach to seasonal lake level manipulation may have a positive effect on largemouth bass survival, biologists think. Even though the lake is almost forty years old, it continues to produce excellent bass fishing that rivals Lake Barkley.

"This is the third year [1982] that the lake level has been held at elevation 359 until about July 4th. In past years the drawdown began around June 15," explained Bill McLemore. "Consequently, a lot of the young-of-the-year bass had to leave the bushes before they were big enough to escape predation. We hope to see stronger year classes as evidence of the benefit of holding the lake level up longer."

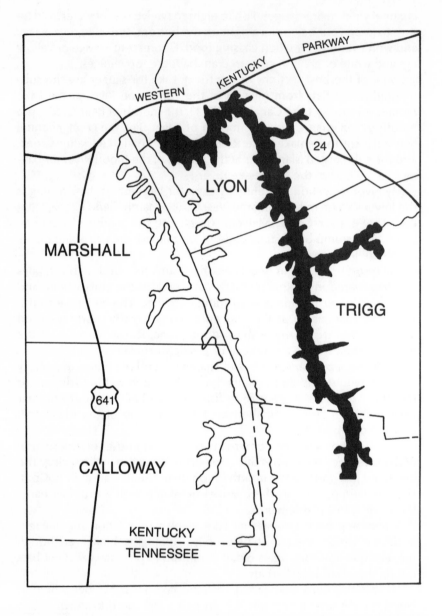

Lake Barkley

Location

Lake Barkley is approximately 30 miles southeast of Paducah in Livingston, Lyon, Caldwell and Trigg counties. The 7,985-foot-long earth and concrete dam with navigation lock, canal and hydro-power generating plant, is at mile 30.6 of the lower Cumberland River.

The lake is accessible via a number of highways—mainly the Western Kentucky Parkway, Ky-80, Ky-164, Ky-1489, Ky-139, Ky-274, Ky-93, Interstate-24 and US-62/641. The cost of the project was $145 million.

Lake Barkley can be found on the following TVA navigational maps: 1101, 1102, 1103 and 1104 in the scale of 1 foot equals ½ mile; or the following topographic quadrangles in 1/24,000 scale: Birmingham Point, Cadiz, Canton, Cobb, Eddyville, Fenton, Grand Rivers, Lamasco, Linton, Mont and Princeton West.

- No-Wake Embayments: None
- Outboard Motor Size Restriction: None

Size

This lake was built under the authority of the Nashville, Tennessee, District of the U.S. Army Corps of Engineers. This 118-mile-long impoundment extends from Dickson County, Tennessee, to Grand Rivers, Kentucky, in Livingston County. Completed in July 1966, Lake Barkley is Kentucky's third largest man-made impoundment.

Lake Barkley is more like a river at flood stage than a lake. There's swift current in the old river channel, and miles of mudflats border the deep water at winter pool. The shallow embayments offer classic structure—humpbacks, stump beds, brush piles and submerged creek channels.

The 57,900-acre lake, 42,020 acres of which are in Kentucky, reaches an elevation of 359 at summer pool; the winter drawdown reduces the lake to 45,210 surface acres at elevation 354. There are 1,054 miles of shoreline at summer pool. Total storage capacity of the impoundment is 93,430 surface acres.

For more information write: Resource Manager, Lake Barkley, U.S. Army Corps of Engineers, Box 218, Grand Rivers, KY 42045, or telephone (502) 362-4236.

Lake Barkley—courtesy of Kentucky Office of Tourism Development

Marinas

There are six marinas on Lake Barkley—Lake Barkley State Resort Park Marina, Prizer Point Marina, Eddy Creek Resort Marina, Kuttawa Harbor Marina, Leisure Cruise Marina and Port Ken Bar Marina.

The Lake Barkley State Resort Park Marina, ½ mile west of the lodge, is open year-round and has 152 slips, 112 of which are covered. Rental boats include 14-foot aluminum fishing boats with 7.5-horsepower outboards, 24-foot pontoon boats with 35-horsepower outboards, and one pontoon boat with a 70-horsepower outboard. Fuel, grocery staples, fishing equipment, live bait (minnows, red worms and nightcrawlers) and limited freezer space for cleaned fish are available. A boat-launching ramp is nearby. For more information write: Lake Barkley State Resort Park Marina, Route 2, Cadiz, KY 42211, or telephone (502) 924-9954.

Prizer Point Marina, 12 miles northwest of Cadiz on Ky-274, is open March 1 to mid-November, weather permitting. There are 81 boat slips, 46 covered and 35 open. The aluminum fishing boats, 14-footers, utilize 9.9-horsepower outboards. The rental fleet of 41-to-45-foot houseboats are powered by 155-to-255 horsepower inboards. Fuel, boat sales and service, live bait (minnows, red worms and crickets), fish-cleaning station, freezer space, boat-launching ramp and fishing tackle are available. For more information write: Prizer Point Marina, Inc., Route 4, Box 219, Cadiz, KY 42211, or telephone (502) 522-3762.

Eddy Creek Resort Marina is 8 miles south of Eddyville on Ky-93. Open March 1 to November 1, the marina has a total of 135 boat slips, 68 covered and 67 open. Sit-down meals or carry-out lunches are available from the marina's restaurant. The rental fleet includes 14-foot fishing boats with 10-horsepower outboards, 24-foot pontoon boats with 50-horsepower outboards, 16-foot bass boats with 25-horsepower outboards and 42-foot houseboats. Off-season rates available. Fishing tackle and licenses, ice, gas, oil and LP gas, fish-cleaning station, freezer space, and boat-launching ramp are available. There are also live bait (red worms, minnows and crickets), boat and motor sales, and outboard motor repair service. For more information write: Eddy Creek Resort Marina, Route 1, Box 327, Eddyville, KY 42038, or telephone (502) 388-7743.

Kuttawa Harbor Marina, open year-round, is 3 miles east of Kuttawa, off US-641/62. The 122-slip marina has rental fishing boats, 14- and 16-footers, equipped with 9- and 18-horsepower outboards, respectively, and 24-foot pontoon boats with 25-horsepower outboards. Fuel, boating accessories, live bait—crickets, minnows and red worms—fish-cleaning station, freezer space, a large assortment of artificial lures, and launching ramp can be found at the dock. A hull-scrubbing service is also available. For more information write: Kuttawa Harbor Marina, Route 2, Kuttawa, KY 42055, or telephone (502) 388-9563.

Leisure Cruise Marina, off US-641/62 on Poplar Creek, is 1 mile west of Kuttawa. Open year-round, the marina has 120 boat slips, 100 of which are covered. Fourteen-foot fishing boats with 7.5-horsepower outboards and 24-foot pontoon boats equipped with 40-horsepower outboards are available. The marina's houseboat fleet includes 45-, 44-, and 38-footers. All houseboats are powered by 130-horsepower Volvo inboards. Boarding time is 3:00 P.M., check-out time, 10:00 A.M.. A deposit is required with reservations; off-season and midweek specials are available. Operating lessons are given free of charge before departure, and deposits will be refunded under terms of the rental contract agreement. The marina has two launching ramps, fish-cleaning station, freezer space and live bait—minnows, crickets and red worms. For more information write: Leisure Cruise Marina, Box 266, Kuttawa, KY 42055, or telephone (502) 388-7925.

The Port Ken Bar Marina at Grand Rivers is reached via Ky-453, ½ mile north of the Barkley Canal. The marina is open year-round, but the boat rentals are offered only from April 1 through Thanksgiving. There are 217 boat slips, 75 of which are covered. Deposits are required for both the 50-foot houseboats and the 24-foot pontoon boats. The rental fishing boats do not have motors. Live bait (minnows, crickets and nightcrawlers), fuel (regular and mixed available at the five-pump fuel dock), fish-cleaning station, freezer space, boat-launching ramp, marine store, artificial bait and tackle are available at the marina. For more information write: Port Ken Bar Marina, Box 162, Grand Rivers, KY 42045, or telephone (502) 362-8364 or 362-8239.

Fishing

There's no doubt in my mind that Kentucky's top major impoundment for largemouth bass fishing is Lake Barkley.

It didn't take long for the fishery to develop once the gates were closed on Barkley Dam in 1966 and the Cumberland River bottoms were flooded. Those first few years were simply amazing—limits of bass could be taken in no time with little more than a cane pole and a glob of wiggling nightcrawlers jigged in submerged brush on the flats.

Barkley Dam—courtesy of Kentucky Office of Tourism Development

Cover was abundant, and small bass were everywhere in numbers that staggered the imagination. A classic flatland reservoir, Lake Barkley, during those first few years, ranked right up there with such famous bass impoundments as Lake Eufaula, Toledo Bend and many others throughout the South.

Lake Barkley is still something special to bass anglers in Kentucky, but it's no secret that the bass fishery has been in a slow decline due to the disintegration of cover, increased turbidity caused by the presence of growing numbers of bottom-feeding rough fish, more competition for available food, decreased fertility, and increased fishing pressure. Such are the population dynamics of man-made impoundments—the first few years are super and then the fishing levels off.

Perhaps it can best be said that Lake Barkley has reached a junction in this cycle of development. Today, the sprawling, shallow impoundment undisputedly continues its reign as the king producer of trophy largemouths. Quality strings of bass are there for the taking, for the angler who sticks with it and isn't intimidated by the fact that it's not as easy as it used to be.

A fish attractor program initiated by the Kentucky Department of Fish and Wildlife Resources in cooperation with the U.S. Army Corps of Engineers has greatly increased available cover and improved fishing throughout the lake. The summer of 1982 marked the end of five years of work on the east bank of the lake. Deep-water brush pile attractors were placed in Dry Creek, the Little River embayment, Eddy Creek, Donaldson Creek, Dryden, Hurricane and Lick Creek embayments.

At Lake Barkley, if you're in a brush pile, you're likely to be on fish, eight to nine months out of the year. But an important thing to remember is don't just fish the shoreline cover. It's a common mistake many anglers make on this impoundment. There's just as much fish-holding structure, maybe more, in the open-water areas!

During spring, the best bet is the jig and pork rind combination (pork frogs, split tails or ripple rinds) on deep points, or plastic worms (black or purple) fished across stump rows along drop-offs. Crankbaits in the lighter natural finishes, or black and white, chartreuse, or yellow-skirted spinnerbaits work best as the fish head into stickups in the flats, as the water warms.

Spinnerbait expert Joe Mickey DeMoss of Madisonville suggests fishing the east side of the lake in Dryden, Little River, McNabb and Hurricane Creek when the water's up in the buck bushes and willows during May and June. DeMoss makes the Brushmaster spinnerbait and markets it and other lures through the Moss Lure Company, Box 46, Hanson, KY 42413, telephone (502) 322-3357.

"I like to fish a ¼-ounce chartreuse spinnerbait with twin copper blades. Just cast it back in the heavy cover on the shady side. Anytime the water's above 55 degrees during this time of year and you've got a foot and a half of water, you're gonna have bass. It's just a matter of finding them," DeMoss explained.

In summer, fish the brush piles and other submerged cover with surface lures early in the morning and at dusk. The Lunker Lure buzzbait and floating-diving lures like the Rapala are used extensively. Be sure to work the cover thoroughly. Motor oil or blue plastic worms, jigs (doll fly and shad types) and spinnerbaits work best during the day. DeMoss suggests flippin' as a top technique during the hot, still days of June. "Plastic worms and jig and worm combinations seem to work best."

During autumn, the rocky points and steep bluffs on the east bank of the lower end of the lake (between Eddyville and mile 38 of the Cumberland River) are fished with darker natural-finish crankbaits. Position the boat so that you're casting parallel to the bank. Spinnerbaits are tops along stump rows, and worms continue to produce fish from the edges of creek channels in heavy cover (don't overlook fish attractors).

As fall fades into winter, bass begin their trek back into the deepest water of the old river channel and the mouths of the major tributary channels. Since the lake is extremely shallow at winter pool (elevation 354), bass vacate the flats and concentrate in sixteen to twenty-four feet of water.

Money Cliff, at river mile 39, is one of my favorite spots on the lake for fishing in November, December and January. I feel the same about late fall fishing as I do early spring fishing. It's a time to catch "wall hangers." The great part about fishing Lake Barkley in the autumn is that you'll darn near have the water to yourself. Everyone's in the woods of Land Between the Lakes bowhunting for deer!

After the fall drawdown, turbidity from barge traffic and low water (playing havoc with access to some areas of the lake) hamper fishing. Black bucktail jigs are the ticket to winter bass on Lake Barkley; the split tail and pork chunks seem to work best.

There are several embayments of the impoundment where I have consistently caught bass. My favorite is Mammoth Furnace Bay, at river mile 49, on the west bank. The mouth of the creek is a tangle of submerged channels, stump rows and humpbacks. It's a crankbait and worm fisherman's paradise! The embayments of Carmack and Demumbers also have classic structure, flats adjacent to stump-lined creek beds. There are also a great many old roadbeds in this section of the lake, which are best fished with Rebel Wee-R crankbaits in bone or crayfish patterns.

Bass from Lake Barkley—courtesy of Kentucky Office of Tourism Development

Crappie are also a major fishery of Lake Barkley. At a crappie fishing seminar in Gilbertsville in October 1980, Western District fish biologist Bill McLemore, of Kentucky's Department of Fish and Wildlife Resources, revealed some incredible findings of a creel survey conducted from mid-April 1978 to mid-March 1980 on Lake Barkley.

McLemore said that "the white crappie occupied 63 percent of more than 1,818,000 pounds of fish harvested on 752,000 fishing trips [a total of 3,294,000 hours on the water]," adding that the months of April and May accounted for 50 to 70 percent of the white crappie harvest.

Sauger, white bass, rockfish and channel catfish are also important fisheries in Lake Barkley, but the impoundment is a bassman's dream come true. The fact still remains that if you want bass, it's not that tall an order to fill. Night fishing the flats with a plastic worm or buzzbait is highly effective.

With all the hundreds of bass tournaments held on the lake each year, and all the thousands of bass caught, you'd think the lake would be suffering from too much fishing pressure. But I still think the lake is underfished. It's so productive, and there's so much fish-holding structure. Lake Barkley is just amazing!

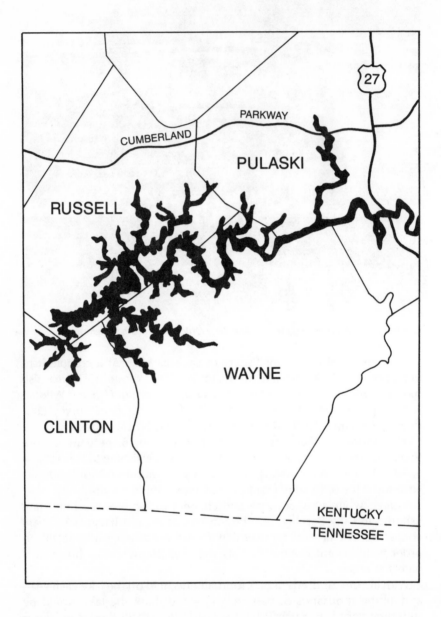

Lake Cumberland

Location

Lake Cumberland is approximately 100 miles south of Lexington in Whitley, Laurel, Pulaski, Wayne, Russell and Clinton counties. Built under the authority of the Nashville District of the U.S. Army Corps of Engineers, it is accessible via many highways, mainly Interstate-75, Cumberland Parkway, Ky-80, US-127, Ky-196, Ky-92, US-27, Ky-789, Ky-834 and Ky-76.

Completed in 1952, Lake Cumberland is fed by numerous creeks and springs which help to keep the lake cool, and clear enough to make fishing difficult. The lake is a mountain impoundment which winds its way through the Cumberland Plateau. The headwaters of the lake are near Burnside, at the western boundary of Daniel Boone National Forest, and Wolf Creek Dam is eight miles south of Jamestown, reached via US-127.

The U.S. Geological Survey topographic quadrangles in 1/24,000 scale for the lake are Burnside, Cumberland City, Delmer, Eli, Faubush, Frazer, Jabez, Jamestown, Mill Springs, Nevelsville, Parnell, Russell Springs, Somerset and Wolf Creek Dam.

- No-Wake Embayments: None
- Outboard Motor Size Restriction: None

Size

The 101-mile-long lake with 1,255 miles of shoreline is Kentucky's largest. (While Kentucky Lake and Lake Barkley are larger in total size, parts of both lakes are in Tennessee.) At summer pool, Lake Cumberland has about 50,250 surface acres and reaches an elevation of 723 feet above sea level; the winter drawdown reduces the lake to 35,823 surface acres at elevation 673.

Lake Cumberland is also one of Kentucky's deepest lakes, more than 180 feet just above the dam. The average depth is 91.2 feet, and the volume of water in the lake is estimated at 6,089,000 acre-feet.

Tree-covered knob hills are the backdrop for this impoundment. The steep rock cliffs which extend along most of the shoreline give the lake fjordlike grandeur. From the air, the lake is simply beautiful as it widens west of Mill Springs. Its serpentine path contours rolling hills, and at sunset the azure waters glisten, highlighting rocky islands, once mountaintops, which jut from the cool depths.

For more information write: Resource Manager, Lake Cumberland, U.S. Army Corps of Engineers, Box 450, 1000 Boat Dock Road, Somerset, KY 42501, or telephone (606) 679-6337.

Marinas

There are 10 marinas on Lake Cumberland—Lake Cumberland State Resort Park Marina, Burnside Marina, Buck Creek Dock, Grider Hill Dock, Beaver Creek Marina, Jamestown Dock, Alligator Dock 1 and 2, Conley Bottom Resort Marina and Lee's Ford Dock.

Lake Cumberland State Resort Park Marina is approximately 14 miles southwest of Jamestown off US-127 and has a large fleet of rental houseboats. Reservations may be made either by mail or by phoning. A deposit is required for confirmation ten days after the reservation is made. The 50-, 53- and 58-foot houseboats can be rented either by the week or for a three-day weekend.

Seasonal prices are in effect on weekends between May 1 and Labor Day. Off-season, weekend rates are reduced up to 30 percent. In addition, a four-day "middle of the week special" (Monday through Thursday) features houseboat rentals at reduced prices—30 percent off the weekend prices, even after Labor Day. This means that during the middle of the week off-season, the rate is a full 60 percent off the seasonal price for weekends.

All rental houseboats are fully carpeted and come with grills, flush toilet, lavatory, deck chairs, dishes and linens, 3-burner gas range, icebox and cooler. The boats sleep eight; renters should bring their own blankets and pillows.

The 14-foot fishing boats with 15-horsepower outboards and 16-foot pontoon boats with 35-horsepower outboards may be rented at both daily and hourly rates. Complete live bait, tackle, snack bar and boating supplies are available. The marina also has 150 open slips and a launching ramp. For more information write: Lake Cumberland State Resort Park Marina, Box 21, Jamestown, KY 42629, or telephone (502) 343-3236.

Burnside Marina is on Lakeshore Drive, just south of Burnside off US-27. The marina ia open twenty-four hours a day in the summer and 8:00 A.M. to 4:00 P.M. November 1 to March 31. There are 148 covered slips, tackle, live bait, snacks, launching ramp and fish-cleaning table. Rental boats include 14-foot aluminum fishing boats with 15-horsepower outboards, 22-foot pontoon boats with 35-horsepower outboards and houseboats. For more information write: Burnside Marina, Box 577, Burnside, KY 42519, or telephone (606) 561-4223.

Buck Creek Dock is the farthest upstream of all facilities on Lake Cumberland. Eight miles south of Somerset on Ky-769 at Haynes, Kentucky, the dock is open April 1 to October 31. Buck Creek Dock is a mile from its confluence with the Cumberland River, just north of the Daniel Boone National Forest boundary. The dock has 35 covered slips, launching ramp, snacks, fish-cleaning table, regular gas, live bait (minnows and nightcrawlers) and tackle. For more information write: Buck Creek Dock, Box 28, Somerset, KY 42501, or telephone (606) 382-5542.

Grider Hill Dock is 10 miles north of Albany off US-127 on Ky-734. There are 150 covered slips and the dock is open twenty-four hours a day during the summer, daylight to dark during the fall, winter and early spring. There's a fish-cleaning station, freezer space, live bait sales (worms, nightcrawlers and minnows) and a boat-launching ramp. The rental fleet includes 14-foot fishing boats with 7-to-20-horsepower outboards and 40- and 52-foot houseboats. Off-season rates are 25 percent off and midweek specials are available. Gas isn't included in houseboat rental costs. For more information write: Grider Hill Dock, Route 4, Albany, KY 42602, or telephone (606) 387-5501.

Beaver Creek Marina is reached by driving 9 miles northwest from Monticello on Ky-92, then 1 mile on Ky-674. The marina, open year-round, has 30 boat slips. The 14-foot fishing boats are equipped with 10-horsepower outboards. Live bait (minnows and nightcrawlers) snacks and boating supplies are sold at the dock. Freezer space and a fish-cleaning station are available. For more information write: Beaver Creek Marina, Route 3, Monticello, KY 42633, or telephone (606) 348-7280.

Jamestown Dock is 3 miles south of Jamestown off Ky-92. The 100-slip marina is open twenty-four hours year-round. Live bait and a complete line of tackle are available. Rental boats include 14-foot fishing boats with 15-horsepower outboards and 50- and 54-foot houseboats. There's a fish-cleaning area and freezer space at the dock. For more information write: Jamestown Dock, Route 2, Jamestown, KY 42629, or telephone (502) 343-3535.

Alligator Dock 1 is approximately 10 miles southeast of Russell Springs, reached via Ky-80, Ky-76 and Ky-1383. Open seasonally, April 1 through November 1. The rental houseboats range in length from 40 to 55 feet. The rental fleet also includes 26- and 32-foot pontoon boats and 14-foot aluminum fishing boats with 5.5-horsepower outboards. Gasoline, snacks, live bait, tackle and artificial lures are also available at the dock. For more information write: Alligator Dock 1, Route 5, Box 261, Russell Springs, KY 42642, or telephone (502) 866-3634.

Lake Cumberland—courtesy of Kentucky Office of Tourism Development

On adjoining property to Alligator Dock 1, Alligator Dock 2, open year-round, twenty-four hours a day seasonally, has 146 slips, 108 of which are covered. The rental houseboats are 58-footers with gas grills and showers. Off-season rates are available. Both 32-foot pontoon boats and 14-foot aluminum fishing boats with 5.5-to-9.5-horsepower outboards are available. Facilities include a fish-cleaning station, freezer space, snack bar, grocery, and boating and fishing supply sales. For more information write: Alligator Dock 2, Route 5, Box 269, Russell Springs, KY 42642, or telephone (502) 866-6616.

Conley Bottom Resort is 8 miles north of Monticello on Ky-1275. The Marina is open twenty-four hours a day in the summer and from 6:00 A.M. to 8:00 P.M. weekdays and 6:00 A.M. to 10:00 P.M. on weekends during the off-season. There are more than 50 covered slips at the marina. Rentals include pontoon boats, 24- and 34-footers, 14-foot fishing boats with 6-to-18-horsepower outboards and 46-foot houseboats. Midweek and off-season rates are available. Fuel, tackle and live bait, boating supplies, and fish-cleaning area and freezer space are available at the dock. For more information write: Conley Bottom Resort, Box 90 A, Monticello, KY 42633, or telephone (606) 348-6351 or (606) 348-8328.

Lee's Ford Dock, 6 miles west of Somerset off Ky-80, has 100 boat slips. There's a grocery store and buoy lines for overnight or long-term moorings. The dock is open year-round, twenty-four hours a day in the summer. The rental 14-foot aluminum fishing boats are equipped with 9.9-horsepower outboards. The pontoon boats can be rented at both daily and hourly rates. Both 43- and 50-foot houseboats rent by the week. Tackle, snack bar, fuel, live bait (minnows and nightcrawlers) and boating supplies are available. The restaurant is open seasonally, March to November. For more information write: Lee's Ford Dock, Box 753, Somerset, KY 42501, or telephone (606) 636-6426.

Fishing

Lake Cumberland enjoys a special status among Kentucky's major lakes. Not only is the impoundment our largest but the list of fishes that inhabit its waters is impressive indeed. Yet many anglers seem to find a way to criticize Lake Cumberland for one reason or another.

Today, the outlook for Kentucky's third oldest impoundment is brighter than ever because of the emergence of a new major sport fishery, the walleye; the reestablishment of the rainbow trout; and the presence of record-class rockfish.

It's now clear that the reason the rainbow trout fishery declined, and eventually disappeared, was the loss of habitat—water of the temperature and with levels of dissolved oxygen that fulfilled the critical requirements of these cold-water fish. The loss of suitable water was directly linked to the lowering of the lake's level so that repairs could be made on a section of the earthen dam that was leaking.

By 1980 the hole in the dam was plugged, and the lake's level returned to its normal seasonal pools. The fishery is now being reestablished through limited stockings. Cutbacks in the federal budget have made it difficult to come up with the funds needed to raise enough fish for the continued stocking of Kentucky's trout waters—streams, tailwaters and lakes—in addition to the thousands and thousands of trout needed for Lake Cumberland. At one time there simply weren't enough fish to go around, but the problem is being solved.

The rainbow trout (*Salmo gairdneri*) is primarily an open-water fish, and can be taken by deep-water trolling, casting spinners during the cold months of the year in and around feeder streams, or still-fishing shad minnows, nightcrawlers, corn niblets or cheese at night over gas lanterns. The area above the dam near the mouths of Otter, Beaver and Indian creeks is a top rainbow haunt.

The best fishing news at Lake Cumberland in some time is the re-emergence of a walleye fishery. For ten years after Lake Cumberland was impounded, native populations of walleye that were in the old river grew to enormous size, offering many trophy-class individuals. In 1958, a 21-pound, 8-ounce fish, believed to be the third largest walleye ever taken in the United States, was caught from Lake Cumberland.

But biologists soon realized that the walleyes were of the so-called southern strain, and were unable to reproduce in their new lake environment. The monster walleye were simply "holdovers," grown fat and sassy on abundant forage but not able to sustain their numbers. Hence, the fishery died out.

In 1973, northern strain walleye fry, hatched at the Senecaville National Fish Hatchery at Lake Pymatuning on the Ohio-Pennsylvania border, were stocked in Lake Cumberland. "Since the start of the project, we've stocked 3,329,000 one-to-two-inch walleyes in Lake Cumberland, and almost one-third of that total was in 1980," said Benjy Kinman, predator fish biologist for the Kentucky Department of Fish and Wildlife Resources, Division of Fisheries.

The year 1981 was an important one to the walleye program. The stockings ended, and Kinman shifted his efforts toward the evaluation of natural recruitment. The spawning run in the headwater streams—Rockcastle, South Fork of the Cumberland, Laurel River and the main fork of the Cumberland River—was studied, as well as the reproduction occurring on rocky shoals and riprap in the main lake.

"One good point about the northern strain walleyes is that they will definitely spawn in the still-water environment," said Kinman. "We've used gill nets to catch mature adults in the main lake, in conjunction with the tagging of mature adults during the spring run."

Another important part of the study is evaluating the exploitation rate of adult fish through a mark and recapture study. Through the use of tags, which biologists are requesting anglers to return by mail, the numbers of fish caught can be monitored.

Walleye favor the gravel flats and rocky points along the main river channel, especially those adjacent to the string of small islands that flank deep water between the dam and river mile 20. Nightcrawlers fished on a Lindy Rig and backtrolled across the extensive flats at the mouth of

Cleaning crappie from Lake Cumberland—photo by author

Beaver Creek are a sure bet for walleye action. Fish the Rapala Count-down, Bagley's Deep Lip Shad, Rebel Shad, and Thin Fin Shad across the deep points, since walleye seem to prefer threadfins as forage in Lake Cumberland.

Further cutbacks in the budgets of federal hatcheries could curtail stockings of the northern strain walleyes in Lake Cumberland, but Kinman said the Division of Fisheries has taken steps to counteract such losses. "We've already proved we can electrofish mature walleye from the headwater rivers of Lake Cumberland, strip them of their eggs and milt, and hatch off the fry at the Minor Clark Hatchery," he said. "That's one of the major reasons the hatchery was built, to bolster our walleye programs across the state."

Other fish that understandably get considerable attention on Lake Cumberland are the black basses—the smallmouth, largemouth and spotted. The lake is usually clear and boat traffic can at time make fishing difficult, but there are several key approaches that seem to pay off handsomely.

The key to successful bass fishing during the first few months of the year can best be summed up as concentrating on embayments where there's runoff water entering the lake. A deep, relatively cold impoundment, Lake Cumberland warms up slowly in the spring. Explains Freddie York, the Russell County conservation officer for the Kentucky Department of Fish and Wildlife Resources, "There's often as much as a six-to-eight-degree difference in water temperature from the mouth of a bay to its shallow headwaters. During the late afternoons of early spring days, the runoff from wet-weather creeks can warm up the back ends of these bays considerably."

Flooded timber, willows, drift piles and stump beds at the back ends of bays are particularly productive places to fish in the spring. While the smallmouth and spotted bass are abundant in Lake Cumberland, the largemouth seems to dominate the creel during April, May and June. Strangely enough, the largemouth disappear when hot weather sets in, perhaps dispersing after the spawn and suspending, because they are taken consistently during the summer only by anglers who cast the banks at night in shallows off the main channel. During the warm-weather months, spotted bass and smallmouth are caught more frequently, as they congregate on deep, rocky points of the main lake. This pattern continues into the fall, until real cold weather sets in.

A major drawdown of the lake between 1968 and 1977, which was necessary to repair a leak in the earthen section of Wolf Creek Dam, allowed many of the shallow back bays to grow up in willows and saplings, much to the advantage of the largemouth. Fishing Creek is one embayment that was overgrown with willows when the water level returned to normal. The tremendous success of the spring '81 bass spawn has been attributed as much to high and stable water conditions as to the abundance of cover, which is so important in holding down predation on the fry and fingerlings.

Because virtually all of the land surrounding Lake Cumberland is heavily forested, there are few local sources of silt, although muddy water conditions do occur because of conditions upstream. In the spring, the lake has good color, especially in the backs of bays where runoff enters. During the summer, the lake is often too clear to fish except in low light.

Waterfalls are numerous along the shoreline, and often hold big fish in the spring, even though the surrounding water may be deeper and considerably cooler than where the runoff comes into the lake. Runoff water entering the lake will often wash in salamanders, minnows and insects, as well as creating warm pockets of water that attract bass in the spring. If you're going after numbers of bass, fish these warm-water pockets.

The John Sherman Cooper Steam Plant, near Burnside, discharges warm water into the lake year-round. White bass, spotted bass, walleye, sauger and largemouths congregate in the area at various times of the year. Spoons, spinnerbaits and crankbaits all are effective when fished in the area. Black basses seem to be drawn to the area in the fall and early spring, while white bass and rockfish congregate there in the winter.

A fish attractor program was initiated on Lake Cumberland in the late 1970s. Both brush piles and storm-downed trees were placed in the lake. The attractors are in Pitman, Fishing, White Oak, Indian, Beaver, Otter and Indian creeks, and the sites are marked by small wooden fish which are nailed on trees along the bank, adjacent to the sites.

Generally speaking, the lower thirty-five miles of lake offer the best spring fishing for largemouths. The embayments which have cover most preferred by largemouths are Lily, Greasy, Pumpkin, Clip, Caney and Wolf. While Otter Creek does have many steep rock banks which usually aren't that productive in the spring, it also has several waterfalls and a group of islands with adjoining flats known locally as "Goat Islands." There are also islands and flats in Wolf Creek.

During spring's high-water period, there's plenty of flooded cover in Fishing Creek, as well as submerged roadbeds upstream of the Cumberland Parkway bridge. The old roads provide access by four-wheel-drive vehicle to deer hunting areas after the winter drawdown. There are extensive mudflats and submerged willows in Fishing Creek, which converges with the old river at mile 44. Fishing Creek is my personal favorite bass fishing embayment on Lake Cumberland.

Extensive stands of flooded timber in Greasy Creek usually hold bass in April, but are difficult to fish because of drift. Bass in Lake Cumberland seem to be particularly active after light rains in the spring, especially in the shallows. While lure selection is a matter of personal preference, and generally ones that prove effective on other bass lakes in the spring will catch fish at Lake Cumberland, there are several lures that consistently seem to top the list.

"If you're fishing the head of a bay where a creek flows in, floating stick baits like the Rapala or A.C. Shiner are particularly effective," York explained. High water during the spring often submerges these feeder creeks, giving bass access to undercut banks, bedrock shelves and a glut of forage—bluntnose minnows, darters, crayfish and fingerling sunfish.

"Crankbaits [crayfish colored, bone and orange combinations, and medium-sized chartreuse-colored spinnerbaits] are the most effective spring baits in these shallows," York said. Chartreuse is perhaps the most widely used color in murky water; white and yellow doll fly and pork rind combinations fished in deeper water account for many spring bass.

Generally, deep-water techniques will yield larger fish, but considerably fewer. Plastic worms aren't fished much in the early spring here, although after rains, they can be effective. Because successful spring fishing patterns are so strongly influenced by temperature on Lake Cumberland, fishing pressure is heavy at times in the best embayments. My suggestion for a way to escape this competition, and at the same time perhaps score on larger fish, is to work the main channel dropline.

There are numerous small islands, gravel flats and stump lines along the lower fifteen miles of the channel. These areas consistently hold big fish that cruise the shallows in the spring during warm afternoons, just as they do at night during the hot summer months. Fish deep-running crankbaits and pig and jig combinations slowly and methodically.

My favorite overlooked area on the lake is the west bank of Lowgap Island, locally known as the "cutoff" between Lake Cumberland State Resort Park and the main lake. The narrow, stump-lined channel is usually bypassed by fishermen running full speed to get to the main lake. It's a sleeper, the kind of spot that everyone disregards, yet it has shallows and gravel points, great big stumps, and deep water nearby, just the ticket for catching a big fish when most of the other anglers are boating small ones at the backs of bays.

Lake Cumberland State Resort Park—courtesy of Kentucky Office of Tourism Development

No fishery program in Kentucky has stirred up as much controversy as the stocking of Lake Cumberland with rockfish. Many persons in the area tourism business continue to feel that the fish are bad for the lake. Yet biologists have proven through stomach content studies with netted "stripers" that they don't eat bass, which was one of the major contentions of the opponents of the program. While it is true that the rockfish are preying on some of the stocked trout, their diet is mainly shad, often fish that are too large for bass to eat.

Rockfish are stocked primarily to correct forage imbalances, but they also provide a secondary benefit—a sport fishery. And Lake Cumberland's sport fishery for rockfish has been impressive so far. The impoundment has yielded some huge fish, including Kentucky's state record, a 47-pounder, as well as a remarkable IGFA line-class record striper that weighed 45 pounds, 8 ounces, and was landed on 8-pound test monofilament.

But the jury is still out on the fishery. The program has entered the evaluation stage, and sometime in the mid-1980s the decision will be made on whether stockings of the pure-bred striped (landlocked) bass will continue. At this writing, the fishery appears to be on the verge of exploding, drawing national attention to the impoundment. On Easter Weekend of 1983, April 2–3, the lake was the site of Striperama I, a national rockfish angling tournament sponsored by Stu Tenney's *Striper* magazine.

The one embayment of the lake which consistently produces rockfish is Beaver Creek. Its confluence with Otter Creek is the top area on the lake. The rockfish seem to congregate there year-round, suspending over humpbacks in twenty-five to forty feet of water off islands, mingling around the breakline of the old river channel. I have seen them flash across the graph recorder in pursuit of shad. The fishing techniques that are most used include vertical jigging Blakemore spoons and big bucktail jigs with white ripple-rind pork trailers, trolling magnum Hellbenders and other over-sized crankbaits, and tight-line fishing with live bluegills. Another section of the lake that produces stripers and white bass alike is the John Sherman Cooper Steam Plant, in the upper end of the lake.

The crappie is taken in great numbers from Lake Cumberland too. My favorite area of the lake for crappie is the upper end of Clip Creek, a small embayment between Greasy and Pumpkin creeks. There are many flooded willows along the submerged creek channel and deadfalls in the deep side hollows. At times, Clip Creek also draws white bass, although Pitman, Buck and Fishing creeks are just as good from March through July during the prespawn run, postspawn jumps and night fishing over the old river channel that follows as summer progresses.

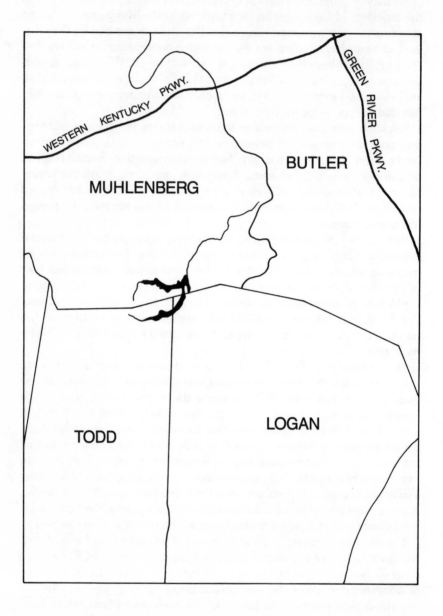

Lake Malone

Location

Lake Malone is approximately 15 miles south of Greenville in Muhlenburg, Todd and Logan counties. Completed in 1961 and opened to the public in 1963, Lake Malone was built by the Kentucky Department of Fish and Wildlife Resources in conjunction with the U.S. Soil Conservation Service.

Lake Malone was impounded from Rocky Creek. The damsite is approximately 11 miles upstream from its confluence with the Mud River. The main access highways to Lake Malone are the Western Kentucky Parkway, US-431, Ky-973, Ky-1293 and Ky-181. Lake Malone can be found on the U.S. Geological Survey topographic quadrangle, in 1/24,000 scale, for Rosewood.

- No-Wake Embayments: None
- Outboard Motor Size Restrictions: None

Size

Lake Malone has 34 miles of shoreline at summer pool and 692 surface acres. The 10-mile-long, wishbone-shaped impoundment has a maximum depth of 40 feet and a mean depth of 20.8 feet.

There's very little fluctuation in the lake's level, since the impoundment's purpose isn't flood control, but recreation. Excess water simply spills over the earthen and concrete dam into the small tailwater area. Total storage capacity of the impoundment is approximately 78 surface acres.

For more information write: Kentucky Department of Fish and Wildlife Resources, 1 Game Farm Road, Frankfort, KY 40601, or telephone (502) 564-4336.

Marinas

There are two marinas on Lake Malone—the Lake Malone State Park Boat Dock and Cherokee Boat Dock.

The Lake Malone State Park Boat Dock is open April 1 to October 31 and has 60 open slips. The 14-foot fishing boats with 5.5-horsepower outboards rent by the hour or by the day. Live bait (minnows, crickets and nightcrawlers), tackle and artificial lures are available, as is mixed gas and a boat-launching ramp. For more information write: Lake Malone State Park Boat Dock, Dunmor, KY 42339, or telephone (502) 657-2111.

The Cherokee Boat Dock is on Ky-1293 off US-431, just southwest of the city limits of Dunmor. Open March 15 through November 1, the marina has 28 open slips. Regular gas, live bait (minnows, crickets and nightcrawlers), hot sandwiches, soft drinks and candy are available at the dock. The rental fishing boats are 14-footers with 6- or 18-horsepower outboards. A fish-cleaning station, freezer space and boat-launching ramp are also available. For more information write: Cherokee Boat Dock, Route 1, Dunmor, KY 42339, or telephone (502) 657-2595.

Fishing

Lake Malone has long been known as a top producer of trophy largemouth bass. After all, it's the largest lake in western Kentucky that's routinely fertilized. The intensive management of Lake Malone also includes weed control when necessary and periodic monitoring of the bass population through electrofishing.

"March and April fishing is especially good," said Southwestern District fishery biologist David Bell. "It's a spring lake." Bell thinks that in

Lake Malone—courtesy of Kentucky Department of Fish and Wildlife Resources

March 1981 the lake may have yielded more big fish than any time in recent years. He said that in the first ten days of March 1981, forty-seven lunkers were taken from the lake. "The fish all weighed over five pounds, and a majority were in the seven-to-ten-pound range," he said, adding that two of the fish topped ten pounds.

The rocky, scenic lake has a maximum depth of 40 feet (at the dam); the mean depth is 20.8 feet. Long and narrow, it has a practically flat bottom with a high shoreline to volume ratio. There are lots of flooded timber and boulders along the shore, deep points, and submerged rock ledges. Lake Malone isn't seasonally manipulated; flood water simply goes over the spillway of the concrete and earthen dam.

The near-constant water level has helped to keep the flooded timber and submerged shoreline brush from rotting away over the years. Loss of cover continues to affect many of Kentucky's major lakes, but not Lake Malone.

The only species of bass found in the lake is the largemouth. To Bell's knowledge, the lake record is an 11-pound, 9-ounce largemouth taken in December 1981. Not only bass are found in Lake Malone but crappie, channel catfish, bluegill and redear sunfish (shellcrackers). The crappie run small, but it's not uncommon to catch eight-to-nine-inch bluegill and shellcrackers (*Lepomis microlophus*) from Lake Malone.

In 1976, 14,000 rockfish fry were stocked in the lake, and a few adults are showing up every now and then. Bell said that he thinks the largest rockfish ever caught from Lake Malone was a seventeen-pounder. The "striper" was taken on a plastic worm by a surprised bass fisherman. In the early summer, there are often scattered rockfish jumps in the lake. Forage in the lake is adequate, although the shad spawn of 1979 was lost in a die-off caused by a bacterial disease.

Lake Malone is a jig and pork rind fisherman's paradise. The plastic worm is also a top lure, especially at night during the summer. At that time of the year Bell said that water in the comfort range of bass (approximately 72 degres Fahrenheit) is likely to be scattered at different depths throughout the lake because of cold water entering the lake from springs. This is one reason why March and April fishing is so productive on Lake Malone. It is the only time when bass concentrate in water that is easily located and fished.

Lake Malone is perhaps Kentucky's best "small" lake, an excellent alternative for the weekend angler who enjoys fishing different waters. Creel surveys in '76 and '77 yielded 8.9 and 9.1 pounds of bass per acre. Hefty bass spawns in recent years, plus threadfin shad stockings, have helped to promote strong year-classes of fish that should continue to produce many trophy-size bass in the future.

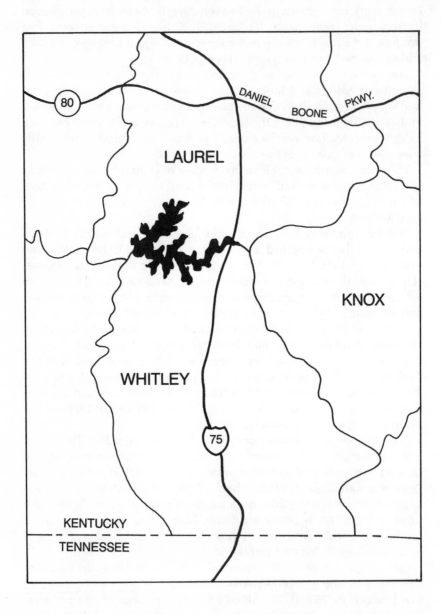

Laurel River Lake

Location

Laurel River Lake is approximately 102 miles south of Lexington in Laurel and Whitley counties. The lake is in the London Ranger District of Daniel Boone National Forest, 15 miles southwest of London, in the Cumberland Plateau. The damsite is approximately 4 miles upstream from the confluence of the Laurel and Cumberland rivers.

This scenic impoundment is accessible via Interstate-75 and US-25W, and several secondary roads—Ky-1277, Ky-192, Ky-363 and Ky-727. Also, three U.S. Forest Service gravel roads—FS roads 611, 62 and 774—provide access to recreational areas (campgrounds and day-use areas) on the northernmost prong of the lake.

Laurel River Lake can be found on the following U.S. Geological Survey topographic quadrangles in 1/24,000 scale: Ano, Corbin, London SW, Sawyer and Vox.

- No-Wake Embayments: None
- Outboard Motor Size Restrictions: None

Size

Built under the authority of the Nashville, Tennessee, District of the U.S. Army Corps of Engineers, the project was opened to the public in the spring of 1974. Construction began in November of 1964. There's no private development on the lake, since the surrounding land is federally owned. The lakeshore is ruggedly beautiful with mixed pine and hardwood forests growing right to the water's edge. There are rocky islands, colorful bluffs, waterfalls and fern-draped boulder fields below the cliffline.

At summer pool, the 19.2-mile-long Laurel River Lake has about 5,600 surface acres and reaches an elevation of 1,012; the winter drawdown reduces this to 4,200 surface acres at elevation 982. The lake has 205 miles of shoreline at summer pool.

Total storage capacity of the impoundment is 6,060 surface acres. The cost of the project was $59.7 million. For more information write: Resource Manager, U.S. Army Corps of Engineers, Laurel River Lake, Route 1, Box 574M, London, KY 40741, or telephone (606) 864-6412.

Marinas

There's only one marina, the Holly Bay Marina, on Laurel River Lake.

The Holly Bay Marina is reached via FS road 611 and Ky-1193. The rental fleet includes 48- and 52-foot houseboats, 16-foot aluminum fishing boats with 10-horsepower outboards and 24-foot pontoon boats with 50-horsepower outboards. Deposits are required on some boats. The marina's restaurant is open on weekends only. Live bait sold at the dock includes red and meal worms, minnows and crickets. Fishing lures, boating supplies, as well as gas, can also be purchased at the marina. For more information write: Holly Bay Marina, Box 674, London, KY 40741, or telephone (606) 864-6542.

Fishing

The rainbow trout has been the number-one fish at Laurel River Lake since it was built. The deep, cold lake is ideal for this cold-water "second-story fishery," although there are limited populations of warm-water species—largemouth bass, spotted "Kentucky" bass, crappie, bluegill and catfish.

The first rainbow trout were stocked in 1973. They were comparatively small fish, four-inchers, and only about 30,000 were stocked. After 1975, the stocking class was increased to 65,000 fish annually, and the individual size increased to about ten inches, setting the stage for the establishment of a strong fishery.

In recent years, all the rainbows stocked in the lake were raised at the Wolf Creek National Fish Hatchery. Ted Crowell, assistant director of Kentucky's Department of Fish and Wildlife Resources, Division of Fisheries, characterizes the rainbow trout fishery "as good to excellent. The local anglers are attuned to the rainbow. They know how to locate and catch him, and they're bringing in some strings of real nice fish."

"Growth rates have been excellent," said Jim Axon, Dingell-Johnson coordinator for the Division of Fisheries. "By autumn, trout stocked in the early spring usually are in the 2-to-3-pound class." Growing fast by gorging on threadfin and gizzard shad forage, the rainbows can be caught by still-fishing at night over gas lanterns using nightcrawlers, kernel corn or cheese, or by deep trolling shadlike crankbaits.

During the winter months, rainbow trout congregate in the shallow feeder creeks and in the open expanses of water just above the dam. Some die-hard anglers often take their limits during this time of the year by spincasting globs of worms or nightcrawlers and spinners in feeder creeks or by trolling shadow-running crankbaits. Be sure to fish the pools of water that collect at the base of waterfalls.

"Rainbows prefer water that's between 54 and 61 degrees Fahrenheit, and during the hottest part of the summer they often become concentrated in narrow bands of this optimum tempertature water at depths over 40 feet," explained Axon. "But during summer nights, when it's cooler, rainbows can be taken by fishing in 15 to 20 feet of water. The fishing has been excellent in the last few years."

"Most fishermen think the larger trout are holdovers from earlier stocking classes, but most of the time they're last spring's fish," said Axon. "To my knowledge, the largest rainbow taken from Laurel River Lake was a 4-pounder." One technique that bears investigation is deep-water trolling with the aid of a downrigger and graph recorder, so popular on the Great Lakes. For the most part, though, the tackle and techniques of the average angler at Laurel River Lake aren't that sophisticated.

Other species of fish that are predominate in the creels of anglers at Laurel River Lake are the bluegill, spotted bass and largemouth bass. The stands of flooded timber scattered throughout the lake offer the best bluegill fishing. Crickets and small jigs are preferred for enticing the big bull "gills" to hit. During the summer months they may be as deep as 20 feet. Rogers Creek is a top embayment for bluegill.

Springtime is, of course, the best time to fish the flooded brush and treetops along the banks for crappie. By talking with local fishermen, I gather that the lake receives very little crappie-fishing pressure. The fish run small due to the combination of the lake's poor forage base and underharvesting.

Another cold-water fish that biologists are attempting to establish is the walleye. In 1974, two million fry walleye of the northern strain, hatched at the Senecaville National Fish Hatchery in Ohio, were stocked in the lake. A study may be done in the future to determine the feasibility of trying to establish a smallmouth bass fishery in Laurel River Lake. "There appears to be abundant habitat. A few fish are still around from the native population prior to impoundment," said Axon.

"Occasionally smallmouth are taken, but most of the time in new impoundments, the smallmouths just can't compete with largemouths for food and cover, and the young-of-the-year are heavily preyed upon, especially by largemouths."

Laurel River Lake also supports good populations of largemouth and spotted "Kentucky" bass. Local bass expert Gilbert Hodge, of London, said that to the best of his knowledge "the biggest largemouth ever caught from Laurel River Lake was about an 8-pounder." His personal bests for the lake are a 4-pound, 2-ounce smallmouth, and a 5-pound, 2-ounce largemouth.

This is a classic highland reservoir with gin-clear water and deep rock structure, which are intimidating to many bass anglers. I wouldn't be surprised to learn that many bass die of old age each year in this lake. If you look at a hydrographic map of Laurel River Lake, it's amazing to learn that the bottom of the old river channel lies in about 120 feet of water throughout much of the main lake. That's deep! But Hodge explained that rarely does he catch bass deeper than 20 feet.

An exceptionally beautiful lake, Laurel River is one of Kentucky's most scenic along with Lake Cumberland, Cave Run Lake and Dale Hollow Lake. Its miles of undisturbed shoreline (federally owned land in Daniel Boone National Forest) give it the appearance of the wilderness lakes of Minnesota, Michigan and Ontario, Canada.

There are stunning cliffs, waterfalls, rocky islands, pine forests, huge boulders submerged along the banks and, most important, no summer cottages or condominium resorts whatsoever. In autumn, the lake is

Pre-impoundment view of Laurel River Dam—courtesy of Kentucky Department of
Fish and Wildlife Resources

just breathtaking, a real escape for the angler who doesn't want to cast
his brains out all day and enjoys taking some time to explore the
surroundings.

As in most mountain lakes, spring is about the only time bass anglers
get to fill their stringers with regularity. "During March and April the
fishing is excellent. The bass can be found in 4 to 10 feet of water,
sometimes shallower. I have the most success with a black doll fly and
pork rind combination, and a white spinnerbait," Hodge explained. The
series of humpbacks along the main river channel, just above the dam,
is the place to be in April.

"During the summer they stick out of the water, and grow up in
weeds. It's ideal in the spring. The bass are thick in those flooded bushes.

Photo by Soc Clay

The tops of the humpbacks become shallow flats adjacent to the deep water," Hodge said, adding, "just think how the bass react to a spinner-bait buzzing through those shallows, and you can imagine how good the fishing gets at times."

Simply stating that Laurel River Lake is deep is somewhat of a half truth. The banks aren't straight up and down. There's gobs of structure in less than 10 feet of water—shallow breaklines extending from islands, stands of flooded timber in just about every embayment, and points where the timber was bulldozed prior to impoundment.

The plastic worm consistently produces fish here. Given the abnormally clear water, night fishing is especially productive. My favorite embayment of the lake to bass fish is Craigs Creek. June through August fish the points in 15 to 20 feet of water, Hodge suggests. "I fish the Bushwacker spinnerbait at night, and sometimes a black doll fly." From mid-September through October, spotted bass gang up in schools and chase schools of shad in the open water near the Flatwoods boat launching ramp. "I fish top-water lures such as the Cordell spot or Boy Howdy when the jumps start," Hodge explained. The school fish usually run in the pound-to-pound-and-a-half range. Another top artificial lure on Laurel River Lake is the Model-A Bomber. It's just as effective when trolled in open water for trout as it is on bass when cast across rocky points on summer nights.

The bottom line on Laurel River Lake is that its forage base is inadequate. The super-cold winters in the late '70s virtually wiped out the threadfin shad population, and severely limited the numbers of gizzard shad as well, at a time when the lake's fisheries were expanding. The timing was unfortunate, and the consequence is that the lake hasn't really produced the numbers of fish it should have.

The management strategy for the lake in the mid-1980s is to reestablish the forage base. In 1981, threadfin shad from Arkansas were placed in the lake, since the availability from Lake Cumberland and Herrington Lake was not good. "It's cost prohibitive to net threadfins. We'll strike out completely for a couple of years, then do well the next. What happens is that it costs us lots of man-hours and money, and the results are spotty," Crowell said.

The forage problems are going to have to be corrected before there can be any further work on reinforcing the populations of predator fish—mainly walleye and smallmouth bass. To add to the problems, Laurel River Lake's water isn't very fertile compared to that of other major Kentucky lakes. Through aggressive movement, however, the impoundment will no doubt offer better angling opportunities for warm-water fishes in the future than it does now.

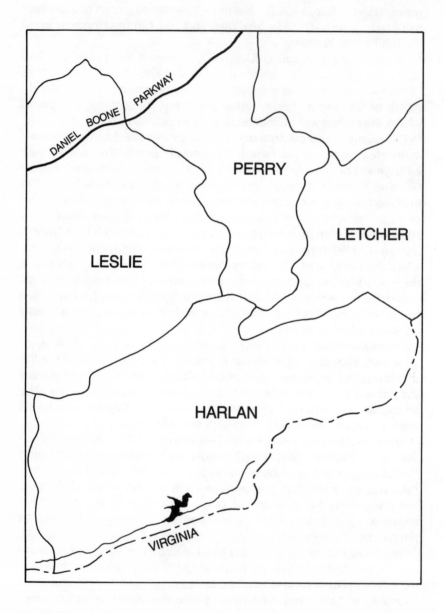

Martins Fork Lake

Location

Martins Fork Lake is approximately 4 miles southwest of Cawood in Harlan County, adjacent to Cranks Creek Wildlife Management Area. This scenic mountain lake was impounded from Martins Fork of the Cumberland River and Cranks Creek, which meet in the upper end of the impoundment.

Located in a flat valley on the Kentucky-Virginia border, the damsite is at river mile 15.6. Construction on the 97-foot-high concrete gravity dam was initiated in December 1973, and the project was put into operation in January 1979. Built by the Nashville, Tennessee, District of the U.S. Army Corps of Engineers, the lake cost an estimated $20.3 million.

The only highway which provides local access to the lake is Ky-217, although the primary access highways are US-421, US-58 and US-119. The project was initiated primarily to provide flood control protection to the city of Harlan, which is 13 miles downstream, at the junction of Clover Fork.

The site for Martins Fork Lake can be found on the U.S. Geological Survey topographic quadrangles, in 1/24,000 scale, for Rose Hill, although it should be noted that, apparently by error, the most recent revision of the quadrangle in 1978 doesn't even show the outline of the lake.

- No-Wake Embayments: None
- Outboard Motor Size Restriction: All watercraft are limited to 10-horsepower motors or less

Size

The drainage area of Martins Fork Lake is 55.7 square miles. At summer pool, the 3.7-mile-long impoundment has 340 surface acres, at elevation 1,310. At flood pool, Martins Fork Lake reaches elevation 1,341. This lake is easily the highest in elevation (Laurel River Lake is the next highest at elevation 1,012) of the sixteen man-made impoundments profiled in this book.

Yet, it's also the smallest in surface acreage. The winter drawdown reduces the lake to 274 surface acres at elevation 1,300. Total storage capacity of the impoundment is 578 surface acres, or 21,100 acre-feet.

For more information write: Resource Manager, U.S. Army Corps of Engineers, Martins Fork Lake, Smith, KY 40867, or telephone (606) 573-7655.

Marinas

There is no marina on Martins Fork Lake.

Fishing

Martins Fork Lake has the unique distinction of being the only impoundment in Kentucky known to have a population of redeye bass (*Micropterus coosae*). These bass closely resemble smallmouth (*Micropterus dolomieui*) in color and body shape.

In *The Fishes of Kentucky*, by William M. Clay, redeye bass are described as having "upperparts dark green, the sides without markings or with obscure traces of the vertical bands characteristic of the juvenile stage, the ventrolateral scale rows with longitudinal dark streaks, the belly whitish. Tip of opercle with a large dark spot. Sides streaked with blue. Median fins, except spinous dorsal, reddish with light margins in young."

Named for the river system from which it was first described, the coosa bass has a geographic range that extends from the Coosa River system in Georgia, through the Alabama River system in Alabama, the Chattahoochee River system in Alabama and Georgia, the Savannah River system in Georgia, to the upper Cumberland River system in Kentucky.

This southern cousin of the largemouth bass was taken on three occasions during samplings of Martins Fork of the Cumberland River and its tributaries in July and August of 1961 by a field party of the Kentucky Department of Fish and Wildlife Resources led by the late James R. Charles. It is believed that at one time the redeye bass was widely distributed in the Tennessee and Cumberland river basins.

The IGFA all-tackle world record redeye bass weighed 8 pounds, 3 ounces, and was taken from the Flint River in Georgia on October 23, 1977, by David A. Hubbard. At this writing, there isn't a redeye bass listed with Kentucky's record fishes. Apparently, any legal redeye bass would be a record fish.

Redeye bass don't adapt to lake environments well, and most of the fish in Martins Fork Lake seem to congregate on riprap, or where there's streamlike substrate. The redeye bass is similar to the smallmouth, and to some extent the spotted bass, in its preferred foods and cover

Martins Fork Lake—courtesy of Resource Manager, Martins Fork Lake

selection. Thus, the angling techniques and lures that are successful for smallmouth and spotted bass work well on redeye bass. Through telephone interviews I got the impression that there aren't many anglers that fish for redeyes exclusively.

Still-fishing "soft craws" and nightcrawlers on deep, rocky points is a tried and true live-bait technique that will entice redeyes to strike. Small "Arkie" jig and pork rind (1⅞-inch by ¾-inch frogs and split tails) combinations, Mepps spinners, "fuzzy grub" jig and live minnow combinations, Sassy Shad, Mister Twisters and four-inch plastic worms, Texas rigged with ¹⁄₁₆-ounce slip sinkers, are all effective on the Martins Fork Lake bass.

The impoundment is unique in that it's the only one in Kentucky where anglers have an opportunity to creel four distinct species of bass.

Eastern District fishery biologist Kerry Prather said that while it's been proven through electrofishing samples that the redeye bass is present in the lake, they aren't found in great numbers. Also, because their growth rate is much slower compared to the largemouth (this is also true for the smallmouth and spotted bass), the redeye bass doesn't commonly reach 12 inches (legal size limit) this far north in its geographic range. "The largest redeye bass I've ever shocked up was about 10½ inches," Prather said.

The largemouth bass is also emerging as a major fishery in Martins Fork Lake. There were approximately 40,000 fry stocked in the lake in May 1979, and Prather said that "14-to-15-inch largemouths were taken during the summer of 1982." During September 1979, 136,000 bluegill fry were also placed in the lake.

It must be stressed at this point that the impoundment is a relatively new one in which the fishing hasn't yet peaked. It is a clear lake, with a flat gravel bottom and scattered stands of flooded timber. The planning of the lake was excellent, as the trees left in the lake bed are in shallow water adjacent to the old river channel. Also, numerous fish attractors were placed in the lake prior to impoundment. "They were all pyramids of tires, anchored to the bottom," Prather said.

A few big largemouths are being taken from Martins Fork Lake, and they are apparently fish that were in the numerous ponds inundated by the lake. The forage base was weak, so gizzard shad were stocked in the lake. Natural forage includes darters, shiners and minnows of various species.

The tailwaters of Martins Fork Lake are a real sleeper for big walleyes. Fish stocked in the Cumberland River in the late 1970s seasonally migrate upstream to the dam, where they congregate in the tailrace from late January through March.

Live nightcrawlers fished on a Lindy rig, ¼-to-⅜-ounce jigs and crankbaits can all be fished easily in the relatively shallow tailwater area, which is only about 12 feet deep in the channel. Plans call for the stocking of rainbow trout in the tailwaters during the spring of 1983.

Between 1979 and 1981, approximately 340,000 walleye fry were stocked in the lake, and they're coming along well. "The walleye are growing rapidly in Martins Fork Lake. This October [1982] I shocked up a 19-inch fish," Prather said.

When fishing Martins Fork Lake, be sure to check out the 219-acre Cranks Creek Lake, which is reached via the access road to the resource manager's office, off Ky-219. "Cranks Creek Lake has a great largemouth bass fishery. It surprised me the last time I electrofished it, monitoring the population," Prather explained.

Dave Csanda with spotted bass—photo by author

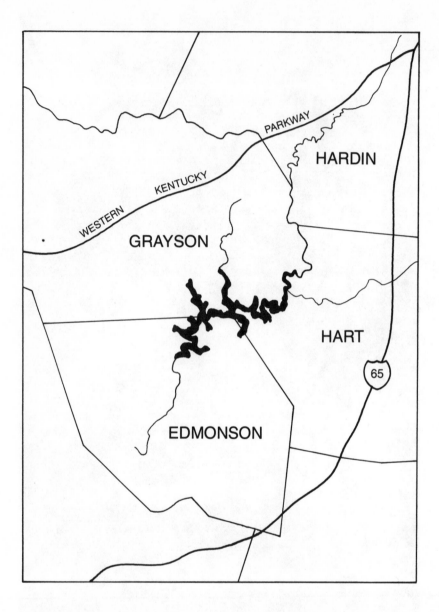

Nolin River Lake

Location

Nolin River Lake is approximately 85 miles south of Louisville in Edmonson, Grayson, Hardin and Hart counties, and can be reached via US-62, Western Kentucky Parkway, Interstate-65, Ky-728, Ky-479 and Ky-88.

If you choose to drive west from Elizabethtown on the Western Kentucky Parkway, rather than take Interstate-65 to Munfordville, take Ky-259 south from Leitchfield. The damsite is 7.8 miles upstream from the Nolin River's confluence with the Green River.

Nolin River Lake can be found on the following U.S. Geological Survey topographic 1/24,000 scale quadrangles: Clarkson, Cub Run, Millerstown and Nolin Lake.

- No-Wake Embayments: None
- Outboard Motor Size Restrictions: None

Size

At winter pool, elevation 490, the lake has 2,070 surface acres. The summer pool is 5,800 surface acres at elevation 515. Approximately 39 miles long, Nolin River Lake has 172 miles of shoreline. The lake controls runoff from a 703-square-mile area.

Nolin River Lake was built under the authority of the Louisville District of the U.S. Army Corps of Engineers. The project cost was approximately $15 million. Construction began in January 1959, with completion coming in March 1963.

For more information write: Resource Manager, U.S. Army Corps of Engineers, Nolin River Lake, Brownsville, KY 42210, or telephone (502) 286-4511.

Marinas

There are three marinas on Nolin River Lake—Wax Marina, Moutadier Boat Dock and Ponderosa Fishing Camp Marina.

Wax Marina is 15 miles south of Clarkson on Ky-88. Open twenty-four hours a day year-round, the dock has 96 boat slips, 52 of which are

covered and 14 especially for houseboats. Fourteen-foot aluminum fishing boats with 7.5-horsepower outboards, 24-foot houseboats and 18-foot pontoon boats are available. Gas (regular and mixed), ice, fishing tackle and bait (crickets, red worms and minnows) can be purchased at the dock. For more information write: Wax Marina, Wax, KY 42787, or telephone (502) 242-7205.

Moutadier Boat Dock is 12 miles south of Leitchfield off Ky-259. Open March 1 through mid-November from 6:00 A.M. to 10:00 P.M. and on weekends the rest of the year, the marina has 300 boat slips, 20 of which are covered. The rental 24-foot pontoon boats are equipped with 40-horsepower outboards; the 17-foot bass boats with 50-horsepower outboards; and the 14-foot fishing boats with 7.5-horsepower outboards. Live bait, fishing tackle, fish-cleaning station, and freezer space for guests are available. For more information write: Moutadier Boat Dock, Box 221, Route 6, Leitchfield, KY 42754, or telephone (502) 286-4069.

Ponderosa Fishing Camp Marina is 13 miles south of Clarkson, reached via Ky-88 and Ky-889. Open April 1 to November 1, 6:00 A.M. to 10:00 P.M., the marina has 50 boat slips, 25 of which are covered. The 14-foot fishing boats with 7.5-horsepower outboards can be rented by the day. There's a boat-launching ramp, fishing tackle, candy, soft drinks and sandwiches. Live bait (minnows, worms and nightcrawlers) and gas are also available. For more information write: Ponderosa Fishing Camp Marina, Route 2, Box 307, Clarkson, KY 42726, or telephone (502) 242-7215.

Nolin River Lake—courtesy of U.S. Army Corps of Engineers

Fishing

Nolin River Lake has always had a reputation for seasonally excellent bass fishing. It is best known as a producer of spotted (Kentucky) bass first and largemouths second, with a smallmouth fishery that's third now but may blossom in years to come. The spring white bass run and an emerging walleye fishery are also much heralded.

Cover is more than adequate in the lake, with a wide array of structure and bank types—steep, rocky walls, "broke" rock points, fallen logs and drift, standing timber, stump beds, brushy, flooded shoreline and shallow flats adjacent to deep channels.

Nolin River Lake is very similar to Rough River Lake. It is a bit higher in elevation, with much more rock structure, and is also much deeper, while Rough River Lake is a better producer of largemouth bass.

Nolin holds some special fishing memories for me. I caught my personal best largemouth bass from the lake when I was a junior at Western Kentucky University in 1971. The 6-pound, 2-ounce large-mouth sucked in my Pedigo Hornet spinnerbait as I bumped it along the bottom with a steady retrieve past a submerged log.

I'll never forget the look on Keith Turner's face when he grabbed that bass by its lower jaw and hoisted it into our flat-bottomed aluminum boat. We didn't have a landing net aboard. I can't remember why, except that the night before Glenn Hale, Keith and I had stayed up late drinking beer and playing cards. It only figures that sleepy-eyed, hung-over bass fishermen would forget to bring the landing net when it's needed most!

While apparently there are no longer any threadfin shad in Nolin River Lake—they were the victims, biologists say, of the severe weather in the late 1970s—the numbers of gizzard shad and other forage fishes in the lake are adequate to support a bass fishery that's just a notch below that of Kentucky's top five bass lakes.

The large numbers of spotted bass mean that anglers often catch a lot of undersized fish, but are never at a loss for action. Magazine publisher Terry Nevins, who fishes Nolin frequently, says that fishing the jumps in the fall is the lake's best-kept secret. In an article in his magazine *Fishing Line*, Nevins suggests that "top-water propeller baits like the Cordell Boy Howdy and Rapala are excellent lure selections when the little Kentuckys are schooled up and feeding aggressively on shad."

Spinnerbaits are also a top fall lure, Nevins says. "White, yellow and chartreuse will work best. Make long casts over shallow points, retrieving the spinnerbait steadily just below the surface. Don't forget to work the stumps and timber too just as you do in the spring when the fish are in the grassy shallows," he adds.

Productive waters also include steep rock ledges and points. Nevins suggests that the deeper banks should be worked parallel for better lure coverage. In summer, the lower third of the lake from the mouth of Conoloway Creek to the dam is tops for largemouth. Fish the river channel points especially hard.

In spring, largemouths make their seasonal treks into shallower water. The flooded timber in Rock Creek, stump beds at the mouth of Little Dog Creek and Dog Creek, and channel droplines in the upper section of the lake between the Ky-88 bridge and Bacon Creek produce some nice strings of bass.

If you fish the main lake channel drops and steep banks, in water as deep as 40 feet, you'll find yourself catching a lot of spotted bass, and a few smallmouths. The deep points seem alive with 10-to-13-inch spotted bass, whereas the smallmouth are concentrated in the upper part of the lake above the Ky-1214 bridge.

Walleye are also showing up in the creel with increasing frequency. From the fry and fingerlings stocked between '75 and '77, adults in the five-to-seven-pound range are being taken. Biologists say that the emerging fishery is a culmination of the stocking program and natural reproduction.

A top spot for walleye is the mouth of Conoloway Creek, on the main lake. In the fall, the walleye converge in 8 to 10 feet of water off the rocky points. Population studies conducted on the lake in the autumn of 1982 revealed that there are numerous fish in the 10-to-13-inch sublegal size; biologists estimate that it takes three years for walleyes to reach legal size in the lake.

The peak period of the spring walleye run is when water temperatures reach 56 to 58 degrees Fahrenheit. Of the walleyes stocked between '75 and '77, one year-class was predominant. This is because the availability of fish wasn't good one year, so consequently not many were stocked. The other year a bacterial infection wiped out the fish in transit from the hatchery to the stocking site.

Walleye were also stocked in '80, '81 and '82. About 150,000 fry total were placed in the lake, and their survival and growth will be monitored to assess the potential for future stockings in the lake. The walleye fry were stocked in suitable habitat, areas where mature walleye were netted during population studies. During electrofish sampling of Dog, Rock and Conoloway creeks, 8-to-11-inch walleye were observed and released.

Springtime is the season for the best white bass and crappie fishing on Nolin River Lake. The upper stretches of the lake along the Grayson-Hart county line form the mouth of Bacon Creek to the Ky-964 bridge offer the best white bass angling opportunities during March and April.

Later, in the summer when the shad begin to school up after spawning, white bass are caught from the jumps in the wide shallows at the mouth of Rock and Dog creeks. The deep points of Long Fall Creek yield many walleye during the summer months; likewise, night fishing over gas lanterns with live minnows is a proven method of catching white bass during the warm nights of June and July. Crappie congregate during their spawning run in the timbered coves in Hunting Fork, Rock Creek, Dog Creek and the coves off the main river channel just above the Ky-88 bridge.

Another developing cold-water fishery is the smallmouth bass. Depending on availability, either fry or fingerlings will be stocked in future years. There is some natural reproduction in the lake, and each year a few respectable-sized fish in the three-to-five-pound class are taken from the old river channel and the upper stretches of the lake where it starts to narrow back into a river. This section of Nolin River Lake also yields some excellent catches of flathead and channel catfish to the angler who sets trotlines in the old river channel.

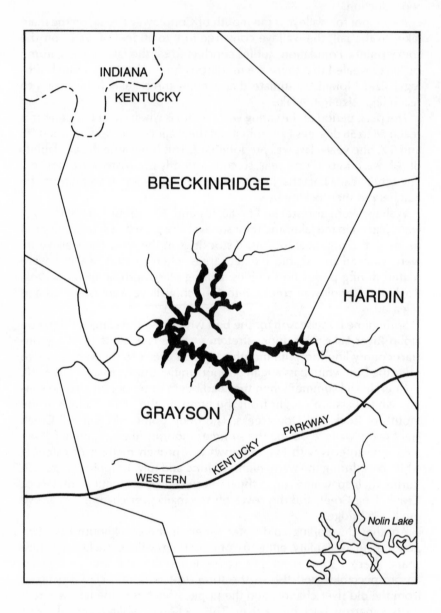

Rough River Lake

Location

Rough River Lake is approximately 67 miles southwest of Louisville in Breckinridge, Hardin and Grayson counties. The damsite is 89.3 miles upstream from the mouth of the Rough River, a tributary of the Green River. Construction began in November 1955, and the project was completed in June 1961.

Rough River Lake is best reached via the Western Kentucky Parkway and Ky-259, although a number of highways provide local access—Ky-79, Ky-108, Ky-110, Ky-1740 and Ky-737. The cost of the project was $9.5 million.

The impoundment can be found on the following U.S. Geological Survey topographic quadrangles in 1/24,000 scale: Custer, Kingswood, McDaniels and Madrid.

- No-Wake Embayments: None
- Outboard Motor Size Restrictions: None

Size

Rough River Lake was built under the authority of the Louisville District of the U.S. Army Corps of Engineers. Approximately 35 miles long, Rough River Lake has 220 miles of shoreline. At summer pool, there are about 5,100 surface acres of water at elevation 495.

The winter drawdown reduces the lake to 2,180 surface acres at elevation 470. The total storage capacity of the impoundment is 10,260 surface acres; the drainage area above the dam is 454 square miles.

For more information write: Project Manager, U.S. Army Corps of Engineers, Rough River Lake, Route 1, Falls of Rough, KY 40119, or telephone (502) 257-2061.

Marinas

There are two marinas on Rough River Lake—the Rough River Dam State Resort Park Marina and Nick's Boat Dock.

The Rough River Dam State Resort Park Marina is 21 miles north of the Western Kentucky Parkway on Ky-79. Open seasonally, the marina

Rough River Lake—courtesy of Kentucky Office of Tourism Development

has 170 boat slips, 16 of which are courtesy slips for park guests. Aluminum fishing boats, 14-footers with 9-horsepower outboards, and 20-foot pontoon boats are available. Fuel, ice, fishing tackle and bait (nightcrawlers, red worms and minnows) can be purchased at the dock. For more information write: Rough River Dam State Resort Park Marina, Box 1, Falls of Rough, KY 40119, or telephone (502) 257-2311, ext. 300.

Nick's Boat Dock is approximately 5 miles west of McDaniels, near the junction of Ky-259 and Ky-79. The boat dock is open from 6 A.M. until 10 P.M. daily from April 1 through November 30. There are 300 rental boat slips. The rental 28-foot pontoon boats are equipped with 40-horsepower outboards while the 14-foot fishing boats have 7.5-horsepower outboards. Live bait, tackle, fish cleaning facilities and freezer space are available. There's also a grocery store on the dock that sells sandwiches, soft drinks, picnic supplies and boating accessories. For more information write: Nick's Boat Dock, McDaniels, KY 40152, or telephone (502) 257-8955.

Fishing

Rough River Lake offers anglers a mixed creel of warm-water and cold-water fishes—bluegill, catfish, crappie, white bass, largemouth bass, spotted (Kentucky) bass and occasionally smallmouth bass and walleye. Biologists estimate that there's approximately 300 pounds per acre of fish in the lake, based on the most recent population studies done in 1980.

The upper section of the lake, especially near Clifty Creek which flows into the river on the Hardin-Breckinridge county line, produces a few smallmouth bass, although most bass anglers aren't aware of this. This is because the majority of the bass anglers fish in the lower tributaries of the lake near the dam, where they're more likely to catch spotted bass or largemouths. Smallmouth bass are few and far between, but each year there are a few nice ones caught.

Increased pleasure-boat traffic and mounting fishing pressure the last few years from Louisville-area anglers have prompted many local regulars to change their tactics. For example, Donovan Smith, who worked on the lake for years as a water safety officer and is now a guide and part-time free-lance outdoor writer, has several suggestions for anglers. "In the summer, night fishing is considerably more effective. Also, if you can, avoid weekends. There's fewer people on the lake during weekdays."

Rough River Lake can be fairly categorized as a "resort lake," very clear with lots of summer power-boating activities that keep the banks churned up. Since the lake is over twenty years old, much of the shore-line cover is gone, and some of the creeks that flow into the lake are silted.

But Rough River Lake continues to yield many fine strings of bass to determined anglers like Smith, who can adapt tackle and technique to the situation. Smith suggests fishing for bass with spinning gear, 4-to 10-pound test monofilament line and smaller lures. His top lures for the lake are four-inch slider head plastic worms, spinnerbaits, buzzbaits and jigs.

"The points, bridge piers, riprap and rock banks are fished to death. In recent years I have concentrated on fishing scattered stumps or rock piles on flats next to submerged creek channel drops. I have also had good luck fishing the old river channel," Smith said.

On many of Kentucky's lakes, fishing pressure is lopsided. Many species that are readily available, easy to locate and catch, and are of high food value, are neglected. The situation at Rough River Lake is no exception, and more and more anglers are finding that fishing for crappie, white bass or catfish, instead of bass all the time, is a relaxing change.

Crappie and white bass—photo by author

Rough River Lake has both crappie and white bass runs in the head-waters during April. Sometime immediately after the lake was built and filled, there were limited stockings of white bass to bolster native popula-tions. Although the white bass fishing on Rough isn't as good as it is on neighboring Nolin River Lake, considerable numbers of fish are taken on up into the summer by anglers casting the jumps or fishing at night by the light of gas lanterns in the lower lake just above the dam.

Little Clifty, Walter, Panther and Cave creeks all have good cover used by crappie in the early spring staging period and actual spawn. The reason is that during the spring of 1978 high water killed about 350 large trees in the embayments. Biologist David Bell and his crew felled the standing timber and cabled it to the banks, creating a large fish attractor area. Crappie don't run too large in Rough River Lake—usually they're seven to eight inches in length by the third year—but Bell said that judged by man-hours on the lake and numbers of fish taken, the crappie is the number-one fish.

Walleye were last stocked in 1975, although a few are occasionally turning up, mostly in the nets of commercial fishermen, who are re-quired to release them. Some of the walleyes caught by accident are real nice ones, ranging from 10 to 12 pounds. And that's a pretty decent walleye in anybody's book.

For a few local walleye fishermen, and visiting anglers from the Great Lakes states who are accustomed to deep-water techniques, the fishery is a bonanza. The deep drop-offs along the old river channel between the mouths of Walter and Cave creeks yield many fine walleye during the warmer months when the fish seek out cooler water and subdued light. Early in the season (February and March), however, the walleye usually congregate in the headwater shallows.

The standing timber in Rough River Lake is an excellent place to fish for both bass and bluegills. In the rocky sections of the lake there are limited populations of other panfish—longear, green and redear sunfish. Drift fishing with crickets in 10 to 25 feet of water off points in the sum-mer or casting small spinners or flies in shallow, timbered coves before June are both good ways to catch big bluegills in Rough River Lake.

Catfish are also largely neglected in Rough River Lake, but they're certainly plentiful. Bell said that he's seen strings of 150 pounds. "The shelves and humps at the mouth of Cave Creek, and at the junction of the North Fork, yield many big catfish. It's a top spot for jug fishing," Bell said. "Fish in five to eight feet of water beginning in late May." As an indication of just how many catfish there are in the lake, consider that during a two-acre cove study in the summer of 1982, over 100 pounds of channel catfish were collected.

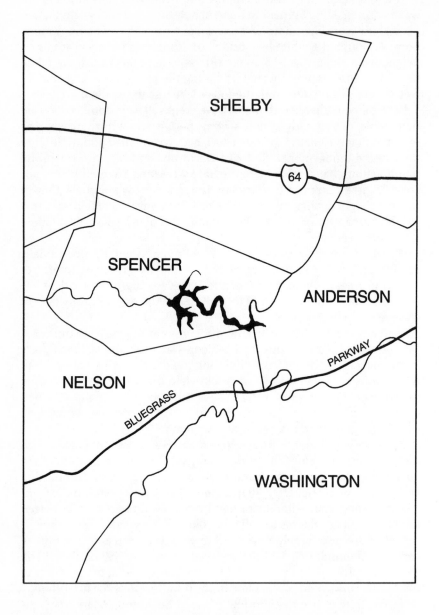

Taylorsville Lake

Location

Taylorsville Lake is approximately 25 miles southeast of Louisville in Spencer, Anderson and Nelson counties. Completed in the summer of 1982 and opened to the public after the seasonal pool was reached, in late May 1983, Taylorsville Lake was built by the Louisville District of the U.S. Army Corps of Engineers.

The lake was impounded from the Salt River. The damsite is approximately 4 miles upstream from the city of Taylorsville, at river mile 60. The main access highways to Taylorsville Lake are the Bluegrass Parkway, Interstate-64, US-31E, US-150, Ky-55, Ky-44, Ky-53, Ky-1066, Ky-1579, Ky-1416, US-62 and Ky-248.

The cost of the project was an estimated $24.8 million. The three-pronged impoundment (which closely resembles Rough River Lake from the air) can be found on the following U.S. Geological Survey topographic quadrangles in 1/24,000 scale: Taylorsville, Chaplin, Bloomfield and Glensboro.

- No-Wake Embayments: None, although the immediate vicinity surrounding Settlers Trace Marina and the Van Buren boat-launching ramp, are no-wake areas. Also, because the lake is extremely narrow in some sections, there are numerous embayments that are off limits to waterskiing.
- Outboard Motor Size Restrictions: None

Size

Taylorsville Lake has 75 miles of shoreline and is 18 miles long at summer pool, elevation 547. The drainage area for the impoundment is 353 square miles. At summer pool, the lake has 3,050 surface acres.

The winter drawdown reduces the lake to 2,930 surface acres at elevation 545. The relatively narrow lake is only 2,000 feet wide at its widest point and 75 feet deep just above the dam. Total storage capacity of the impoundment is 6,350 surface acres.

For more information write: Resource Manager, U.S. Army Corps of Engineers, Taylorsville Lake, Route 2, Box 88, Taylorsville, KY 40071, or telephone (502) 477-5553.

Marinas

While the master plan outlined some $32 million worth of recreational facilities—marinas, boat-launching ramps, campgrounds and day-use areas (scenic overlooks, picnic grounds and day-hiking trails)—construction has been slowed by funding problems.

There are two boat-launching ramps and one marina on Taylorsville Lake. All the facilities are within a 20-minute drive of downtown Taylorsville.

The boat-launching ramp and marina at Settlers Trace is off Ky-44, about three miles east of the city limits, not far by boat or automobile from the damsite. The ramp is wide enough for four or five boats to launch at one time and the parking lot can easily accommodate over 200 automobiles and boat trailers.

The adjacent Settlers Trace Marina has over 125 boat slips, about one-third of which are covered. It is a modern marina with wide walkways, spacious and well-padded slips that is constructed from a steel frame supported by huge plastic foam blocks. There are public restrooms and a water fountain in the retail area.

Rental pontoon boats, 40- and 50-foot houseboats and 14-foot aluminum fishing boats with 15-horsepower outboards are available, as well as ice, snacks, gasoline, fishing tackle and boating supplies.

The boat-launching ramp at Van Buren is off Ky-248 on Ky-1579, approximately 16 miles southeast of Taylorsville. It is located in the scenic, upper end of the impoundment. The lake access area is quite a bit smaller than the Settlers Trace site in terms of parking and ramp size, but nonetheless it's an excellent facility.

Other lake access points are planned for Chowning Lane off Highview Church Road (Ky-1066), Possum Ridge on Ky-1416, and Ashes Creek off Ky-1066.

For a free brochure outlining the rental procedure, what's provided and what to bring, and costs (daily, weekly, four-day package and off-season rates) write: Settlers Trace Marina, Box 336, Taylorsville, KY 40071, or telephone (502) 477-8766 or 477-8776.

Fishing

Taylorsville Lake is an example of how much Kentucky's fishery biologists have learned about impoundment management in the past twenty years.

During the 1960s, when there was a boom in building lakes in Kentucky, rivers were dammed up one after another in rapid succession, and the resulting lakes were opened with little or no preimpoundment

Smallmouth and largemouth bass—courtesy of Kentucky Office of Tourism Development

management planning by biologists, and with few goals related to specific fisheries. While the resulting man-made lakes produced good fishing, it wasn't because of any special management strategy.

Impoundments always offer the best fishing those first few years when optimum cover and good food availability, plus massive spawns and fertile waters, equal exploding fish populations. The population dynamics of man-made impoundments have been extensively documented.

Taylorsville Lake was destined to be different right from the start, an example of how to get the most mileage out of a situation. A great deal has been learned about how fish populations in impoundments are affected by such variables as exploitation by anglers, food availability as it relates to age and growth, various size and creel limits, and the disintegration of cover as it relates to optimum open-water-to-cover ratios.

Taylorsville Lake benefited right from the start from management approaches that have evolved basically through the marriage of increased knowledge and trial-and-error application in the field. Ted Crowell, assistant director of fisheries for the Kentucky Department of Fish and Wildlife Resources, said that "in the planning stages we were looking for a way to give Taylorsville Lake a shot in the arm."

Several steps were taken to maximize the lake's potential and to minimize possible problems right from the start. To minimize the impact of anticipated heavy fishing pressure, since the lake is about a thirty-minute drive from metropolitan Louisville, a fifteen-inch size limit was established on bass. The restrictive size limit helped to postpone heavy harvest until after the population had adequate time firmly to establish itself.

Preimpoundment view of Taylorsville Lake—photo by author

Preimpoundment studies of the Salt River were made to evaluate the species present—game fishes, rough fishes and forage. Their numbers and size range were documented by extensive population samplings. It was found that gizzard shad were present in the river in such numbers that stockings weren't necessary to ensure that there would be good food availability, although Crowell said that eventually threadfin shad may be stocked.

To help anglers concentrate their fishing activity in productive areas, nineteen brush and three truck-tire fish attractor sites were constructed by the contractor during late phases of the preparation of the lake bed. The fish attractors will also help to supplement natural cover, since, unfortunately, in some sections of the lake, trees were simply bulldozed rather than cut down with chainsaws, thus removing all the stumps from channel drops. The fish attractor sites are scattered throughout the lake, although most of them are at the mouths of creeks, cabled to the bottom in fifteen to twenty feet of water. There were no shallow-water sets.

Perhaps the most important aspect of the preimpoundment planning focused on multiple year-class stockings of bass. When the lake reached seasonal pool in the spring of 1983, 15,000 eight-to-nine-inch subadult bass were stocked in the lake. By dividing the surface acreage into the number of bass, we find that the stocking rate is a healthy five fish per acre. All of the bass were hatched and raised at Minor E. Clark Hatchery near Morehead. Also, thousands of fry from the 1983 spawn at the hatchery were stocked in Taylorsville Lake.

Thus, there were three distinct year-classes of bass in the lake at the beginning, since the river supported a small but nonetheless healthy population prior to impoundment. The three-year classes of bass give the lake a marked advantage when it is considered that, in the past, bass populations in our man-made lakes evolved solely from the first year's spawn of adult bass that were present in the river prior to impoundment.

Taylorsville Lake has lived up to its expectations as a productive bass lake. By the summer of 1984, small bass were numerous, but anglers had a problem catching very many 15-inch, legal bass. Holdover fish from the old river in the four-to-six-pound range began showing up in the creel.

Taylorsville Lake has classic bass structure—broad flats, extensive stands of flooded timber along the old river channel and in numerous embayments, weed beds, homesite foundations, roadbeds, submerged farm ponds, fence rows and humpbacks along the old river channel. Stump beds aren't as numerous as in many other lakes, but there are extensive areas of flooded willows in most embayments.

The lake has a mud bottom, with scattered shale outcroppings. Since the lake has very little fluctuation, only two feet between summer pool and winter drawdown, the shoreline cover won't decay rapidly. The discharge below the dam is warm water.

The largemouth bass is the primary sport fish in Taylorsville Lake, and it appears that the spotted "Kentucky" bass won't find the conditions to his liking. Chartreuse, orange, bone and shad pattern crankbaits fished over points and flodded brush on the flats seem to work well in the lake, as well as 6-inch purple, black and firetail plastic worms fished in flooded timber.

Taylorsville Lake also offers some excellent bluegill fishing. Crickets, wax worms and meal worms fished in the flooded timber have yielded some impressive strings of big, adult bluegills. The lake is also expected to produce thriving fisheries of catfish, crappie and white bass, but at this point it's too early to tell.

Dewey Lake

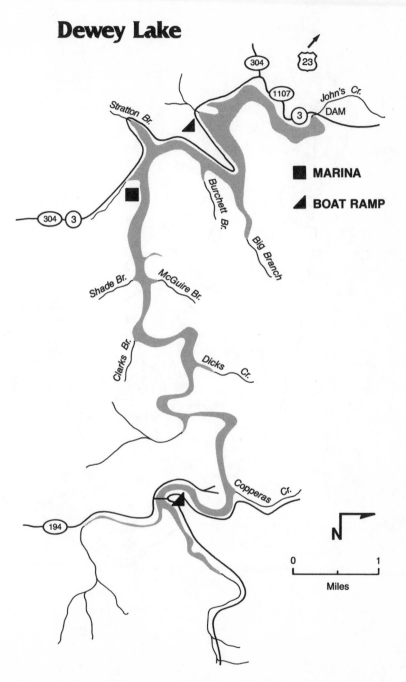

MARINA

BOAT RAMP

N

0   1
Miles

Barren River Lake

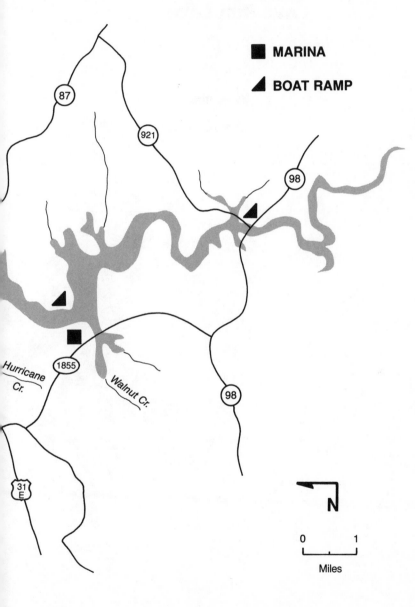

Cave Run Lake

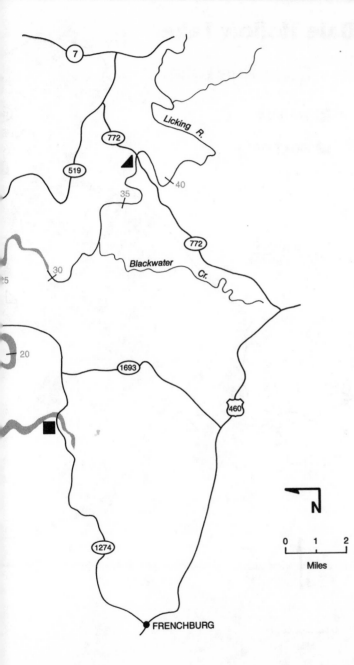

Licking R.

772

519

40

35

772

Blackwater   Cr.

30

25

20

1693

460

1274

N

0   1   2

Miles

FRENCHBURG

7

Dale Hollow Lake

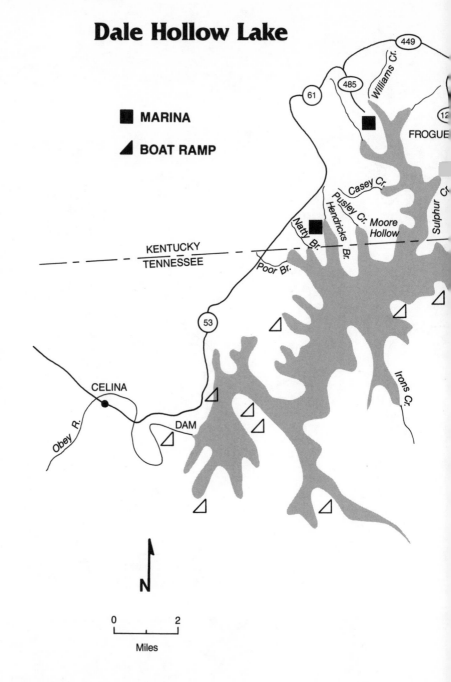

MARINA

BOAT RAMP

KENTUCKY
TENNESSEE

CELINA

DAM

Obey R.

449
485
61
12
Williams Cr.
FROGUE
Casey Cr.
Pusley Cr.
Moore
Hollow
Hendricks Br.
Natty Br.
Sulphur Cr.
Poor Br.
53
Irons Cr.

N

0   2
Miles

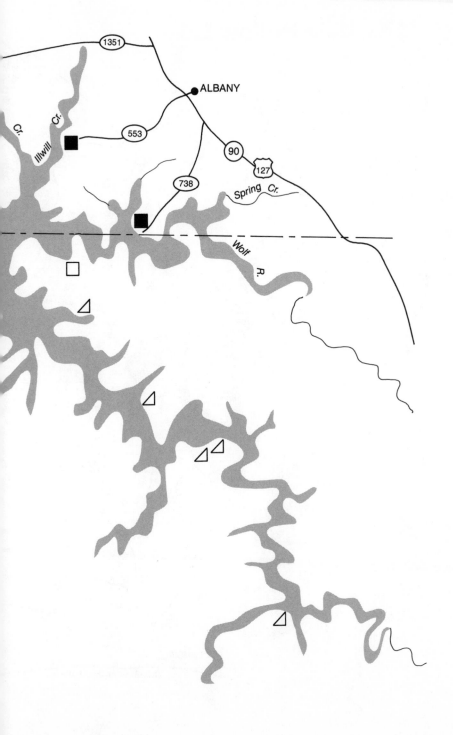

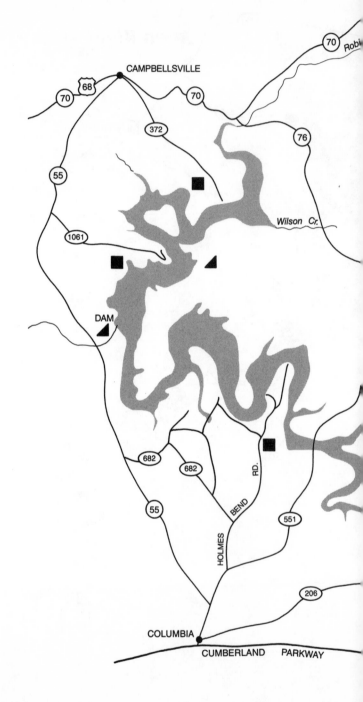

Green River Lake

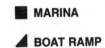

■ MARINA

◢ BOAT RAMP

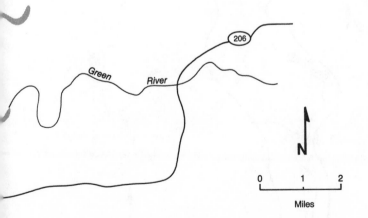

Greenbo Lake

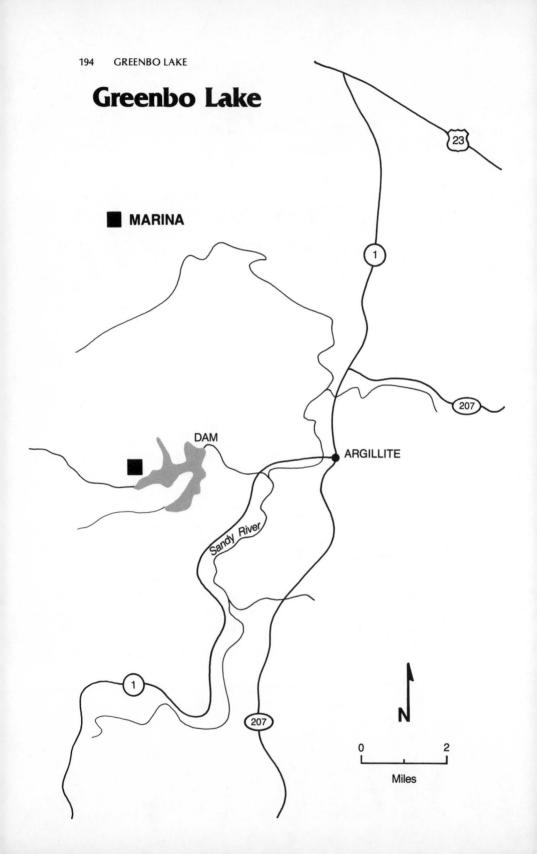

■ MARINA

Lake Malone

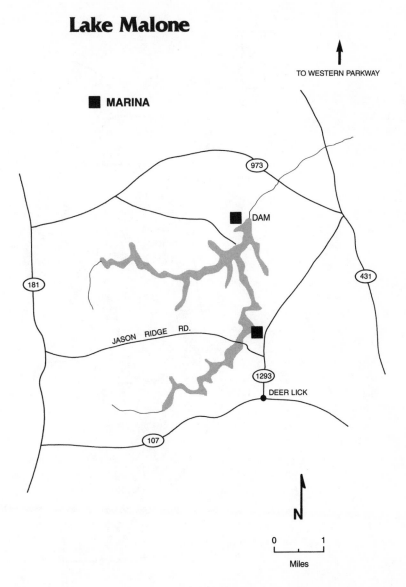

MARINA

TO WESTERN PARKWAY

973

DAM

181

431

JASON RIDGE RD.

1293

DEER LICK

107

N

0   1

Miles

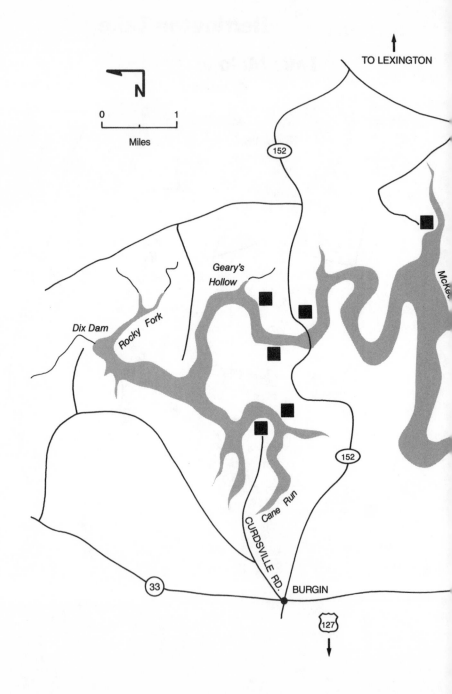

Herrington Lake

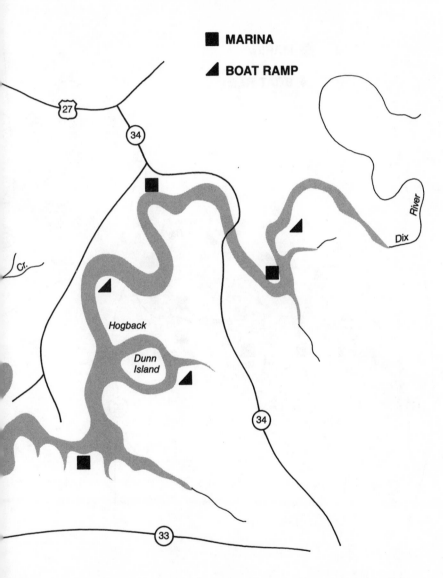

■ MARINA

◢ BOAT RAMP

Kentucky Lake

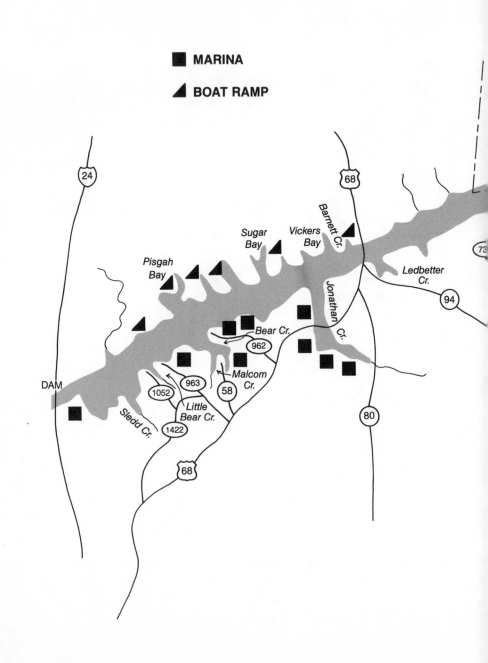

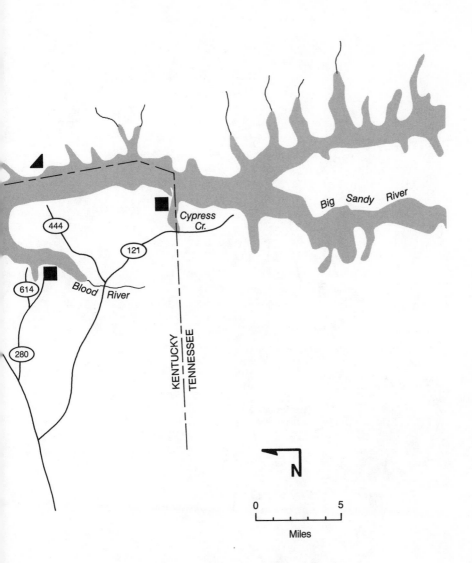

Big   Sandy   River

Cypress
Cr.

444

121

614   Blood   River

280

KENTUCKY
TENNESSEE

N

0   5
Miles

Lake Barkley

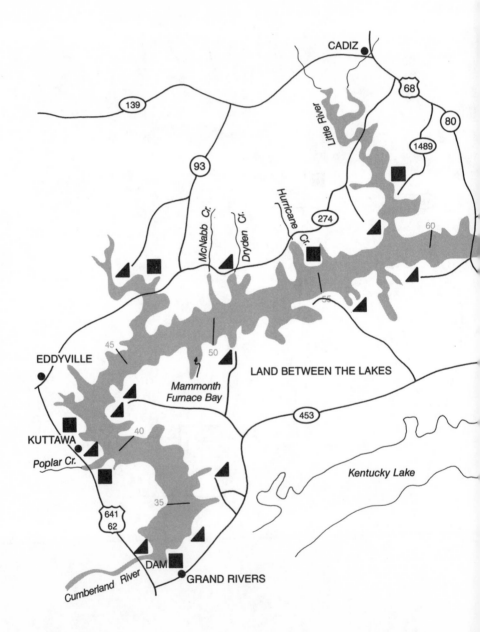

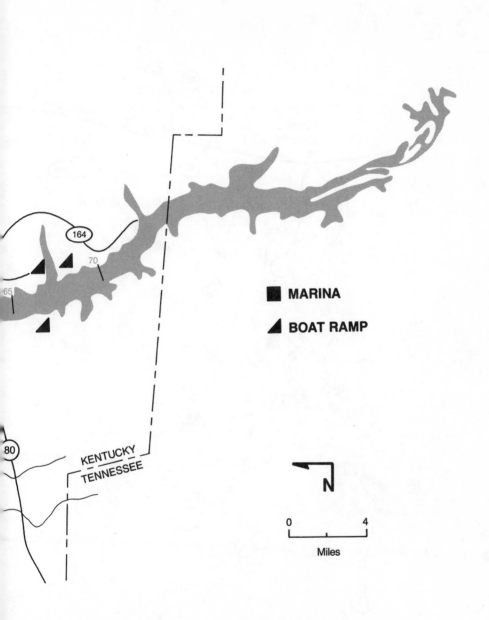

MARINA

BOAT RAMP

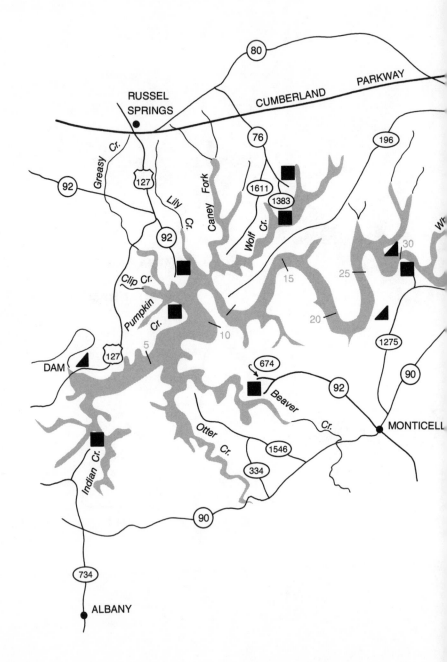

Lake Cumberland

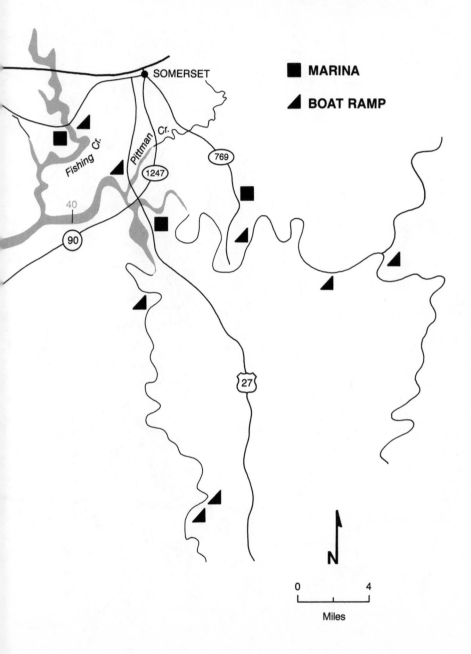

MARINA

BOAT RAMP

SOMERSET

Fishing Cr.

Pittman Cr.

769

1247

40

90

27

N

0   4

Miles

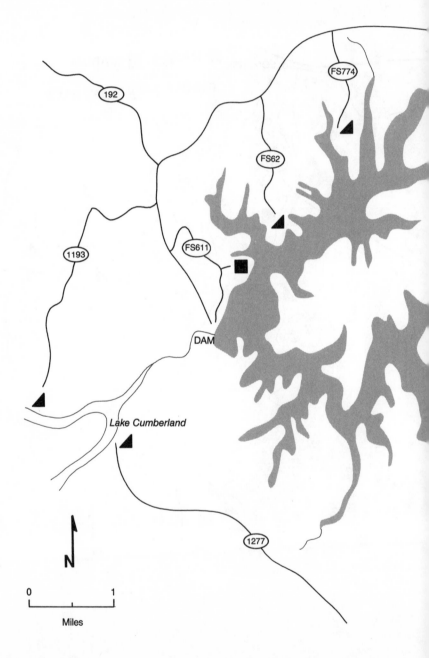

Laurel River Lake

■ MARINA

◢ BOAT RAMP

Martins Fork Lake

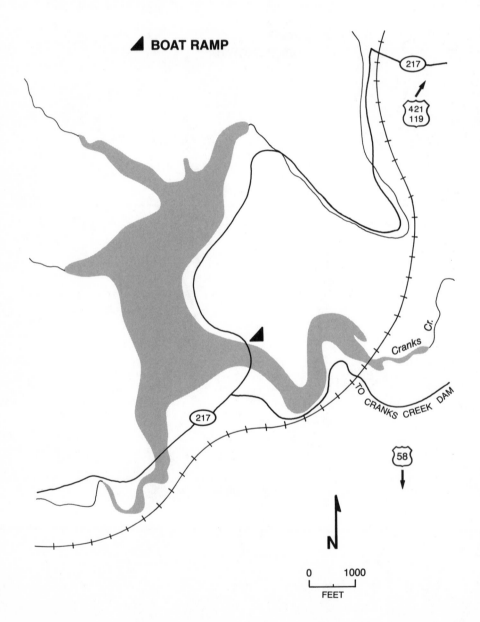

▲ BOAT RAMP

Taylorsville Lake

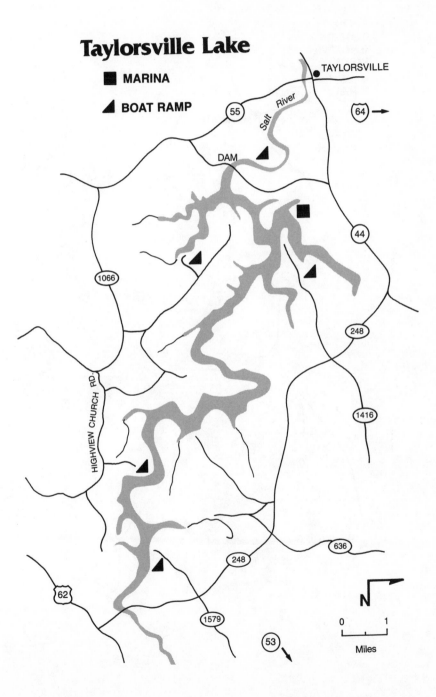

■ MARINA

▲ BOAT RAMP

Nolin River Lake

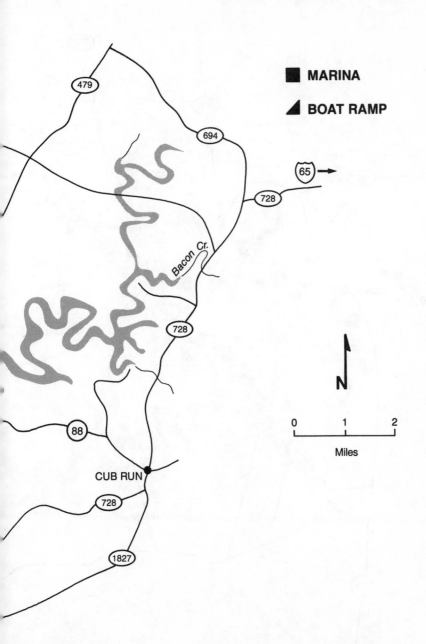

MARINA

BOAT RAMP

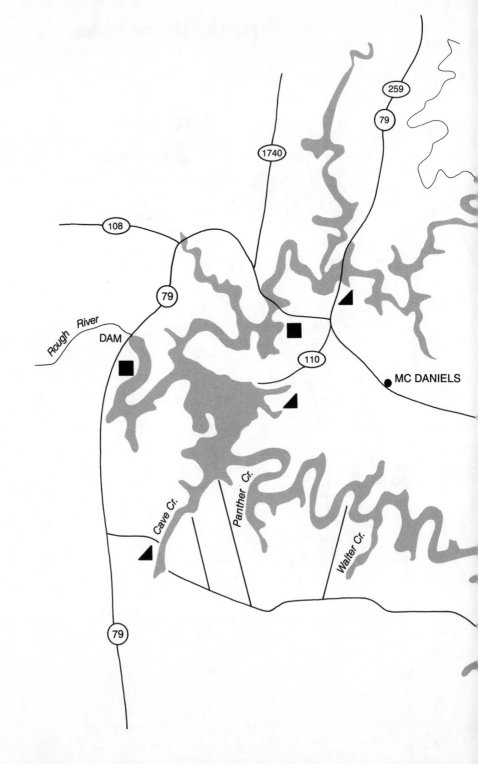

Rough River Lake

Marina Information

Lake	Marina	Season	Address and Phone Number	Boats*
Barren River Lake	Walnut Creek Marina	Open seasonally	Route 4, Box 200C, Scottsville, KY 42164 (502) 622-5858	14-ft. boats (6.5 hp)—$20. 15½- and 16½-ft. bass boats (65 and 75 hp)—$75.
	Barren River Lake State Resort Park Dock	Open seasonally	Lucas, KY 42156 (502) 646-2357	14-ft. boats (7.5 hp)—$20.
	Peninsula Marina	Year-round	Route 2, Glasgow, KY 42141 (502) 646-2223	14-ft. boats (6 hp)—$25 includes one tank of gas. 24-ft. pontoon boats—$70. 42- and 45-ft. house-boats—$150 first day and $100 thereafter. Deposits required on boats.
Cave Run Lake	Scott Creek Marina	Year-round	Cave Run Marinas, Box 174, Morehead, KY 40351 (606) 784-9666	14-ft. boats (9.9 hp)—weekdays, $20; weekends, $25. 24-ft. pontoon boats—$45 to $60. 45- and 50-ft. houseboats—$110 to $135.

Lake	Marina	Season	Address and Phone Number	Boats*
Cave Run Lake	Longbow Marina	Apr.—mid-Nov.	Cave Run Marinas, Box 174, Morehead, KY 40351 (606) 768-2929	14-ft. boats (9.9 hp)—weekdays, $20; weekends, $25.
Dale Hollow Lake	Hendrick's Creek Resort	Mid-Mar.—Oct.	Route 4, Burkesville, KY 42717 (502) 433-7172	14- and 16-ft. boats—$7.50 to $8.50; with 6- to 20-hp outboards—$12 to $17.50. Houseboats—$395 to $1,050 per week. Deposits required.
	Sulphur Creek Marina	Apr. 1—Oct. 31	Star Route 4, Box 39, Kettle, KY 42752 (502) 433-7272	15-ft. boats—$8; with 7.5- to 15-hp outboards—$21 to $26. Houseboats—$415 to $1,025 per week (off-season rates available).
	Wisdom Fishing Camp	Year-round	Route 2, Albany, KY 42602 (606) 387-5821	14-ft. boats (6 to 25 hp)—$15 to $25. Houseboats—$545 to $795 per week.
	Wolf River Dock	Apr. 1—Nov. 1	Route 2, Box 172, Albany, KY 42602 (606) 387-5841	14-ft. boats—$6; with 7.5- to 25-hp outboards—$18 to $24. 23-ft. pontoon boats (35 to 50 hp)—$45 to $50.

Lake	Marina	Season	Address and Phone Number	Boats*
Dale Hollow Lake	Dale Hollow Lake State Park Marina	Apr. 1—Oct. 31	Bow, KY 42714 (502) 433-7490	14-ft. boats (10 hp)—$20. 20-ft. pontoon boats (35 hp)—$60.
Dewey Lake	Jenny Wiley State Resort Park Marina	Year-round	Prestonsburg, KY 41653 (606) 886-2711	15-ft. boats—$4; with 9-hp outboards—$15.
Green River Lake	Holmes Bend Boat Dock	Apr. 1—Oct. 31	Route 1, Columbia, KY 42728 (502) 384-4452	14-ft. boats—$6; with 6-to-9.5-hp outboards—$20. 28-ft. pontoon boats (35 hp)—$65. 40- and 50-ft. houseboats—$475 to $575 per week.
	Taylor County Boat Dock	Mar.—Nov.	Box 282, Campbellsville, KY 42718 (502) 465-3412	14-ft. boats (6 to 7.5 hp)—$20. 40-ft. houseboat—$90 per day or $600 per week.
	Green River Marina	Feb.—mid.-Dec.	Campbellsville, KY 42718 (502) 465-2512	14-ft. boats (9.5 hp)—$22. 24-ft. pontoon boats (40 and 50 hp)—$65. Houseboats—$650 to $850 per week. Deposit required with reservations.

Lake	Marina	Season	Address and Phone Number	Boats*
Greenbo Lake	Greenbo Lake State Resort Park Marina	Apr. 1—Oct. 31	Greenup, KY 41144 (606) 473-7324, ext. 543	14-ft. boats—$3 per hour, $12 per day; with 6-hp outboards—$5 per hour, $20 per day. 18-ft. pontoon boats (6 hp)—$12 per hour, $60 per day. Canoes—$4 per hour.
Herrington Lake	Bryant's Camp and Marina	Apr. 1—Nov. 1	Box 397, Danville, KY 40422 (606) 236-5601	14-ft. boats—$6; with 7.5-hp outboards—$20 (includes one tank of gas).
	King's Mill Marina	Year-round	Route 2, Lancaster, KY 40444 (606) 548-2091	14-ft. boats—$5; with 6.5-hp outboards—$16.
	Gwinn Island Fishing Camp	Feb. 28— Nov. 30	Route 2, Danville, KY 40422 (606) 236-4286	14-ft. boats—$5; with 6-hp outboards—$18 (includes three gallons of gas). 20-ft. pontoon boats (35 hp)—$55.
	Red Gate Camp	Mar. 1—Dec. 15	Route 4, Lancaster, KY 40444 (606) 548-3461	14-ft. boats—$5; with 7.5-hp outboards—$18.

Lake	Marina	Season	Address and Phone Number	Boats*
Herrington Lake	Camp Kennedy Dock	Year-round	Box H, Burgin, KY 40310 (606) 548-2102	14-ft. boats—$7; with 6- or 9-hp outboards—$20. 20-ft. pontoon boats (40 hp)—$65.
	Sunset Marina	Year-round	Route 4, Lancaster, KY 40444 (606) 548-3591	14-ft. boats (5 hp)—$20 (gas included).
	Chimney Rock Resort	Apr. 1—Nov. 1	Route 1, Harrods-burg, KY 40330 (606) 748-5252	14-ft. boats—$6; with 7-hp outboards—$20.
	Freeman's Fishing Camp	Year-round	Route 1, Harrods-burg, KY 40330 (606) 748-5487	14- and 16-ft. boats—$5; with 6-hp outboards—$16.
	Royalty's Fishing Camp	Year-round	Route 4, Harrods-burg, KY 40330 (606) 748-5459	14-ft. boats (6 hp)—$18.
Kentucky Lake	Kentucky Dam Marina	Year-round	Route 1, Gilberts-ville, KY 42044 (502) 362-8500	14-ft. boats (8 hp)—$25. 24-ft. pontoon boats (40 hp)—$15 per hour or $90 per day. 42-ft. houseboats—$600 per week

Lake	Marina	Season	Address and Phone Number	Boats*
Kentucky Lake	Kentucky Dam Marina	Year-round	Route 1, Gilberts-ville, KY 42044 (502) 362-8500	and up (includes 40 gallons of gas); off-season and split-week rates available.
	Moors Resort and Marina	Year-round	Route 2, Gilberts-ville, KY 42044 (502) 362-4356	16-ft. boats—$12 per day, $60 per week; with 6-hp outboards —$22 per day, $110 per week. 26-ft. pontoon boats (40 hp)—$100 per day (seventh day free).
	Big Bear Resort Marina	Apr. 1—Nov. 1	Route 4, Box 156, Benton, KY 42025 (502) 354-6414	14-ft. boats (6 to 15 hp)—$18 to $22. 16-ft. bass boats (35 hp)—$30. 22-ft. pontoon boats—$80 ($40 for a half day).
	Hester's Spot in the Sun Marina	Late Mar.—mid-Nov.	Route 4, Benton, KY 42025 (502) 354-8280	14-ft. boats—$6.50; with 6-hp outboards—$16.50; with 15-hp outboards—$21.50. 25-ft. pontoon boats (50 hp)—$75. Seventh day free on rental boats.
	Will-Vera Village Marina	Mar. 1—Nov. 1	Route 4, Box 228, Benton, KY 42025 (502) 354-6422	14-ft. boats (9.9 hp)—$15. 18-ft. pontoon boats (40 hp)—$65.

Lake	Marina	Season	Address and Phone Number	Boats*
Kentucky Lake	Lakeside Camping Resort Marina	Mar. 1—Oct. 31	Route 5, Benton, KY 42025 (502) 354-8157	14-ft. boats (9.5 hp)—$18. 16-ft. boats (9.5 hp)—$22. 24-ft. pontoon boats (40 hp)—$70.
	Sportsman's Marina	Mar. 15—Nov. 1	Route 5, Box 418A, Benton, KY 42025 (502) 354-6568	14-ft. boats (9.5 hp)—$22. 24- and 28-ft. pontoon boats (50 and 60 hp)—$90. 36- and 42-ft. houseboats—$975 to $1,075 per week.
	Town and Country Resort Marina	Year-round	Route 5, Benton, KY 42025 (502) 354-6587	14- and 16-ft. boats—$7 and $9; with 9.5- or 15-hp outboards—$18 and $23. 24-ft. pontoon boats (40 hp)—$75 ($45 for half day).
	Kenlake State Resort Park Marina	Year-round	Route 1, Hardin, KY 42048 (502) 474-2211, ext. 171	14-ft. boats (9.5 hp)—$22. 24-ft. pontoon boats (35 hp)—$60.
	Blood River Dock	Apr. 1—Nov. 15	Route 5, Murray, KY 42071 (502) 436-5321	14-ft. boats—$4.

Lake	Marina	Season	Address and Phone Number	Boats*
Kentucky Lake	Missing Hill Marina	Apr. 1—Oct. 31	Route 1, CR Box 215A, New Concord, KY 42076 (502) 436-5519	14-ft. boats (9.5 hp)—$16. 25-ft. pontoon boats (40 hp)—$40.
Lake Barkley	Lake Barkley State Resort Park Marina	Year-round	Route 2, Cadiz, KY 42211 (502) 924-9954	14-ft. boats (7.5 hp)—$8 first two hours, $3.50 each additional hour, $20 all day (includes 6 gallons gas). 24-ft. pontoon boats (35 hp)—$30 first two hours, $12.50 each additional hour, $75 all day. Pontoon boat (70 hp)—$35 first two hours, $15 each additional hour, $90 all day.
	Prizer Point Marina	Mar. 1— mid-Nov.	Route 4, Box 219, Cadiz, KY 42211 (502) 522-3762	14-ft. boats—$6; with 9.9-hp outboards—$25. 41- to 45-ft. houseboats—$550 to $850 per week.
	Eddy Creek Resort Marina	Mar. 1—Nov. 1	Route 1, Box 327, Eddyville, KY 42038 (502) 388-7743	14-ft. boats—$10; with 10-hp outboards—$25. 24-ft. pontoon boats (50 hp)—$90. 16-ft. bass

Lake	Marina	Season	Address and Phone Number	Boats*
Lake Barkley	Eddy Creek Resort Marina	Mar. 1—Nov. 1	Route 1, Box 327, Eddyville, KY 42038 (502) 388-7743	boats (25 hp)—$40. 42-ft. houseboats—$895 per week (off-season rates available).
	Kuttawa Harbor Marina	Year-round	Route 2, Kuttawa, KY 42055 (502) 388-9563	14-ft. boats (9 hp)—$19. 16-ft. boats (18 hp)—$23. 24-ft. pontoon boats (25 hp)—$65.
	Leisure Cruise Marina	Year-round	Box 266, Kuttawa, KY 42055 (502) 388-7925	14-ft. boats (7.5 hp)—$20. 24-ft. pontoon boats (40 hp)—$65. 45-ft. houseboats—$800 per week. 44-ft. houseboats—$700 per week. 38-ft. houseboats—$550 per week. $150 deposit required with reservations.
	Port Ken Bar Marina	Year-round (Boat rentals Apr. 1—Thanksgiving)	Box 162, Grand Rivers, KY 42045 (502) 362-8364 (502) 362-8239	14-ft. boats—$10. 24-ft. pontoon boats—$50. 50-ft. houseboats—$450 for 3-day weekend, $450 for 4 days midweek, $750 per week.

Lake	Marina	Season	Address and Phone Number	Boats*
Lake Cumberland	Lake Cumberland State Resort Park Marina	Year-round	Box 21, Jamestown, KY 42629 (502) 343-3236	14-ft. boats—$6; with 15-hp outboards—$25. 16-ft. pontoon boats (35 hp)—$15 per hour, $60 per day. 50- to 58-ft. houseboats—$750 to $1,170 per week, $375 to $585 for 3-day weekend (middle of the week and off-season rates available).
	Burnside Marina	Year-round	Box 577, Burnside, KY 42519 (606) 561-4223	14-ft. boats (15 hp)—$30. 22-ft. pontoon boats (35 hp)—$65 ($75 on weekends). Houseboats available.
	Buck Creek Dock	Apr. 1—Oct. 31	Box 28, Somerset, KY 42501 (606) 382-5542	Boat-launching ramp and gas sales.
	Grider Hill Dock	Year-round	Route 4, Albany, KY 42602 (606) 387-5501	14-ft. boats (7-20 hp)—$21 to $29. 40-ft. houseboats—$115 per day, $630 per week, $380 mid-week. 52-ft. houseboats—$175 per day, $950 per week, $580 midweek (off-season rates available).

Lake	Marina	Season	Address and Phone Number	Boats*
Lake Cumberland	Beaver Creek Marina	Year-round	Route 3, Monticello, KY 42633 (606) 348-7280	14-ft. boats (10 hp)—$20.
	Jamestown Dock	Year-round	Route 2, Jamestown, KY 42629 (502) 343-3535	14-ft. boats (15 hp)—$20. 50- and 54-ft. houseboats—$650 per week.
	Alligaor Dock No. 1	Apr. 1—Nov. 1	Route 5, Box 261, Russell Springs, KY 42642 (502) 866-3634	14-ft. boats (5.5 hp)—$20. 26-and 32-ft. pontoon boats—$75 to $95. 40-to-55-ft. house-boats—$600 to $850 per week.
	Alligator Dock No. 2	Year-round	Route 5, Box 269, Russell Springs, KY 42642 (502) 866-6616	14-ft. boats (5.5 to 9.5 hp)—$20. 32-ft. pontoon boats—$75. 58-ft. houseboats—$750 per week (off-season rates available).
	Conley Bottom Resort	Year-round	Box 90A, Monticello, KY 42633 (606) 348-6351 (606) 348-8328	14-ft. boats (6 to 18 hp)—$20. 24- and 34-ft. pontoon boats—$75. 46-ft. houseboats—$500 to $775 per week (midweek and off-season rates available).

Lake	Marina	Season	Address and Phone Number	Boats*
Lake Cumberland	Lee's Ford Dock	Year-round	Box 753, Somerset, KY 42501 (606) 636-6426	14-ft. boats—$7.50; with 9.9-hp outboards—$19. Pontoon boats—$11 per hour (2-hour minimum), $75 per day. 43-ft. houseboats—$690 per week. 50-ft. houseboats—$780 per week.
Lake Malone	Lake Malone State Park Boat Dock	Apr. 1—Oct. 31.	Dunmor, KY 42339 (502) 657-2111	14-ft. boats—$7; with 5.5-hp outboards—$20 ($7 per hour; 2-hour minimum).
	Cherokee Boat Dock	Mar. 15—Nov. 1	Route 1, Dunmor, KY 42339 (502) 657-2595	14-ft. boats—$7; with 6-hp outboards—$17; with 18-hp outboards—$22.
Laurel River Lake	Holly Bay Marina	Year-round	Box 674, London, KY 40741 (606) 864-6542	16-ft. boats (10 hp)—$30. 24-ft. pontoon boats (50 hp)—$70 ($30 deposit). 48-ft. house-boats—$695 per week. 52-ft. houseboats—$995 per week.

Lake	Marina	Season	Address and Phone Number	Boats*
Nolin River Lake	Wax Marina	Year-round	Wax, KY 42787 (502) 242-7205	14-ft. boats (7.5 hp)—$20. 18-ft. pontoon boats—$50. 24-foot houseboats—$275 per week.
	Moutadier Boat Dock	Mar. 1—mid-Nov.	Route 6, Box 221, Leitchfield, KY 42754 (502) 286-4069	14-ft. boats (7.5 hp)—$25. 17-ft. bass boats (50 hp)—$80. 24-ft. pontoon boats (40 hp)—$75.
	Ponderosa Fishing Camp Marina	Apr. 1—Nov. 1	Route 2, Box 307, Clarkson, KY 42726 (502) 242-7215	14-ft. boats (7.5 hp)—$25.
Rough River Lake	Rough River Dam State Resort Park Marina	Open seasonally	Box 1, Falls of Rough, KY 40119 (502) 257-2311, ext. 300	14-ft. boats (9 hp)—$20. 20-ft pontoon boats—$5 an hour (2-hour minimum), $60 per day.
	Nick's Boat Dock	Apr. 1—Nov. 30	McDaniels, KY 40152 (502) 257-8955	14-ft. boats (7.5 hp)—$20. 28-ft. pontoon boats (40 hp)—$70.

*Unless otherwise noted, rates are per day, gas not included.

Lake	Marina	Season	Address and Phone Number	Boats*
Taylorsville Lake	Settlers Trace Marina	Year-round	Box 336, Taylorsville, KY 40071 (502) 477-8766 or 477-8776	14-ft. boats (15.5 hp)—$25. 40-ft. houseboats—$750 per week. 50-ft. houseboats—$990 per week.

*Unless otherwise noted, rates are per day, gas not included.

Hydrographic Map Outlets

I know of five in-state sources for hydrographic maps of the Kentucky lakes profiled in this book. Unfortunately, it is possible to obtain only line maps for a few of our impoundments, but the situation is improving yearly. It is important to note that U.S. Geological Survey topographic quadrangles (7.5 minute) in 1/24,000 scale don't necessarily show the detail fishermen are seeking. In most cases they show only lake outline.

TVA navigational maps for Kentucky Lake and Lake Barkley (scale: 1 foot = ½ mile), which show lake depth and such lake bed features as stump rows, old homesite foundations and ponds, are available by writing: Kentucky Department of Economic Development, Maps and Publications, 133 Holmes Street, Frankfort, KY 40601, or telephoning (502) 564-4715. Ask for the free booklet "Maps and Publications Price List."

Another source of hydrographic maps for Kentucky Lake and Lake Barkley is Kala Enterprises, Inc., Route 4, Benton, KY 42025, telephone (502) 354-8091. Ed Rezek, a partner in the business, said that the maps measure 2 feet by 3 feet and are four-color with contour lines, structure detail, marina and resort information, plus fishing tips by outdoor writer Wade Bourne. A set of four maps covers both lakes. The Lake Barkley map covers the lower 25 miles of the impoundment. There are three Kentucky Lake maps—north, central and south.

The north section extends from the dam up to the US-68 bridge (Eggners Ferry Bridge), the central section from the bridge to Paris, Tennessee, and the southern section from Paris to Waverly, Tennessee. The maps are $2.00 apiece, plus $.75 each for postage and handling. Rezek said that cash, money orders or checks will be accepted.

Smallmouth bass fishing wizard Billy Westmorland, author of *Them Ol' Brown Fish*, owns and operates a mail-order hydrographic map business that markets maps of Lake Cumberland and Dale Hollow Lake. The maps are color-coded for the best banks to fish for each species seasonally and the recommended lures. Orders are accepted by mail at the following address: Westmorland Maps, Box 310, Smallmouth Road, Celina, TN 38551, or by telephoning (615) 243-2346. The cost for each map is $2.40 plus $.40 postage; his classic smallmouth bass fishing book is $10.95 including postage.

Blue line maps of Herrington Lake, Rough River Lake, Nolin River Lake, Barren River Lake, Lake Cumberland, Greenbo Lake, Taylorsville Lake, Green River Lake, Laurel River Lake and Cave Run Lake are marketed by Angler Graphics, 516 Shaftsbury Road, Lexington, KY 40505, telephone (606) 293-5468. The maps range in cost from $2.00 to $3.50 each, including postage.

The U.S. Army Corps of Engineers is another source of fishing maps. For maps of Barren River Lake, Green River Lake, Nolin River Lake, Rough River Lake, and Cave Run Lake write: U.S. Army Corps of Engineers, Louisville District Office, Box 59, Louisville, KY 40201, or telephone (502) 582-5739. The black and white fishing maps, adapted from 1/24,000 scale topographic quadrangles, sell for $.75 a set (four sheets per lake), postage included.

Maps of Dewey Lake with a scale of 1 inch equals 300 feet are available by writing: U.S. Army Corps of Engineers, Huntington District Office, OAS/Map Sales, 502 8th Street West, Huntington, WV 25701, or telephone (304) 529-5293. The blue line maps are $1.20 each and there are thirteen sheets in the set for Dewey Lake.

Maps of Lake Barkley, Lake Cumberland, Dale Hollow Lake and Laurel River Lake are available by writing: U.S. Army Corps of Engineers, Nashville District Office, Map Section, Box 1070, Nashville, TN 37202, or telephone (615) 251-7271. The Lake Barkley maps are scale 1/5,280, 11 inches by 17 inches in size, and sell for $2.40 a set; the Lake Cumberland maps are scale 1/20,000, 11 inches by 17 inches in size, and sell for $8.00 a set; the Dale Hollow Lake maps are scale 1/20,000, 11 inches by 17 inches in size, and sell for $3.50 a set, and the Laurel River Lake maps are scale 1/12,000, 15 inches by 21 inches in size, and sell for $2.50 a set.

ICON of Kentucky, owned and operated by Charles J. Blaud, 8102 Devonshire Drive, Louisville, KY 40258, produces and markets four-color, large-scale maps of major Kentucky fishing lakes. The details on the maps include underwater contours, fish attractors, stump beds, former building sites and rock formations.

The maps also include basic information such as miles to dam, marinas and recreational facilities. The maps sell for $2.95 plus $.50 for postage and handling. Lake maps available at this time are: Taylorsville Lake, Barren River Lake, Nolin River Lake and Herrington Lake.

The maps can be ordered from: ICON of Kentucky, Box 58275, Louisville, KY 40258, or telephone (502) 937-7017.

Index

About the Author

Arthur B. Lander, Jr., has fished Kentucky's lakes since childhood. He has worked as a summer fishery aide for the Kentucky Department of Fish and Wildlife Resources and frequently covered fishery management topics during three and one-half years as outdoors writer for the *Lexington Herald* newspaper in Lexington, Kentucky.

A free-lance writer-photographer since 1973, Lander is presently writing an outdoor column for *Business First*, Louisville's weekly business newspaper. His travel and outdoor recreation articles and photographs have appeared in a wide variety of other publications, including Exxon's *Vista USA, In-Fisherman, Chevron USA, Southern Living, Outdoor Life, Rural Kentuckian, Odyssey, Deer and Deer Hunting, Southern Outdoors, Turkey Call, Pro Bass,* and *Fishing Line.*

Lander has traveled around the country covering a diversity of outdoor recreation activities. In addition to fishing, Lander enjoys waterfowl hunting, downhill skiing, whitewater rafting and wilderness backpacking. A native Kentuckian, the author lives in St. Matthews, a suburb east of Louisville. This is his third book.

About the author

The following Kentucky titles are available from **menasha ridge press**. Each book is softbound, 6" by 9".

A Fishing Guide to the Streams of Kentucky by Bob Sehlinger and Win Underwood combines the best thoughts and efforts of two of Kentucky's foremost outdoorsmen. Each stream is described with a narrative, a fish profile, a fishing data sheet, and a complete map showing access points. Supplemental chapters provide information on specific species, governing regulations, places to camp, and much more.
ISBN 0-89732-006-9   388 pages

A Canoeing and Kayaking Guide to the Streams of Kentucky by Bob Sehlinger—"Without doubt [Kentucky] has the best and probably the biggest guide to its boatable waters of all the 50 states. . . . In all, about 70 creeks and rivers grace this comprehensive book. . . . The best buy you can make after your canoe, paddle and life jacket."—*Canoe*
ISBN 0-89732-000-X   336 pages

A Guide to the Backpacking and Day-Hiking Trails of Kentucky by Arthur B. Lander, Jr.—"[Lander] has mapped and described in detail approximately 950 miles of country by-ways for backpackers and hikers in Kentucky—231 trails in all. This, quite simply, was an enormous undertaking. . . ."—Louisville *Courier-Journal*
ISBN 0-89732-002-6   322 pages

A Guide to Kentucky Outdoors by Arthur B. Lander, Jr.—"Two national and 17 state parks, 25 lakes, 6 state and 1 national forest and 7 nature and scenic areas are described as potential recreational sites. Opportunities for skiing, scuba diving, hang-gliding, parachuting, and bicycling in Kentucky are also identified."—*Library Journal*
ISBN 0-89732-001-8   280 pages

menasha ridge press
Route 3   Box 450
Hillsborough, NC 27278